The Widows

A Women's Ministry in the Early Church

BONNIE BOWMAN THURSTON

Fortress Press Minneapolis

To honor
Amanda Bryant Kane
and
Ruth Garrison Myers

widows of the church

Library of Congress Cataloging-in-Publication Data

Thurston, Bonnie Bowman.
  The widows.

  Bibliography: p.
  1. Women in Christianity—History—Early church,
ca. 30-600. 2. Widows—Biblical teaching. 3. Widows—
History. I. Title.
BR195.W6T48 1989   270.1'0880654   88–45249
ISBN 0–8006–2317–7

Printed in the United States of America   1-2317
93 92 91 90   2 3 4 5 6 7 8 9 10

Contents

Preface

No one writes a book alone. I am grateful to the following institutions for their assistance: the libraries of Wheeling Jesuit College, Bethany College, Harvard Divinity School, Eberhard Karls University (Tübingen), the American School of Classical Studies (Athens), the British School of Classical Studies (Athens), Cyprus-American Archaeological Research Institute (Nicosia), Institut zur Erforschung des Urchristentums (Tübingen). In addition, I am indebted to Bernadette Brooten, John A. Hollar, Helmut Koester, Linda Maloney, George Miller, Carolyn Osiek, the members of the Women in the Biblical World section of the 1985 national meeting of the Society of Biblical Literature, and especially the Reverend Dr. Burton B. Thurston, Sr., who encouraged this work and provided continuing support, scholarly advice and expertise in ancient languages, and hours of proofreading and fruitful discussion.

Prologue

In recent years much helpful scholarship on women in the biblical world has appeared. Among the many types of studies published have been explorations of the "gender of God" issue, studies of biblical texts dealing with women, reports of archaeological findings, reconstructions of early Christianity, and analyses of parallel literature on the place of women in the ancient world. For centuries, women were omitted from biblical and church history. That omission is now being rectified. But one group of women is still largely ignored: old women. If women were marginal in church history, widows were invisible!

My own observations about widows occasioned this study. In 1983 a number of magazines ran feature articles on the world's fastest growing poverty group: women. In the United States the poorest group of all was elderly women who had been homemakers and who, as widows, had no pensions or health coverage. The statistics I read were particularly striking because I observed in churches I served and visited that it was often this very group of older women who were carrying the primary burden of service to and support of their congregations. I was troubled by the apparent contradiction between the statistics I read and the reality I saw. And so this study was born.

My first line of inquiry was to see how older women were treated in the Bible. What I discovered astounded me. From Israel's earliest days, there was concern for and support of widows. The early Christian church was praised because "there was not a needy one among them" (Acts 4:34), and one of its first benevolent works was for widows (Acts 6:1-7). The church not only supported needy widows but by the second century it elevated them to the status of a clerical order. That order was the most prominent group of women in the first three centuries of the church. The widows as a recognized group were referred to by all of the church fathers and were mentioned in all the major Church Orders. Yet no book-length study had been devoted to the widows and their order.

This book, then, begins by giving a sense of the socioeconomic position of widows in the biblical world. It examines the primary New Testament texts on widows, paying special attention to 1 Tim. 5:3-16. Next, it discusses the references to the widows' order in the Apostolic Fathers, Tertullian of Carthage, and the *Didascalia Apostolorum,* in each case beginning by setting the stage against the larger backdrop of church history. In short, *The Widows—A Women's Ministry in the Early Church* examines the position of Christian widows from the time of Jesus to A.D. 325.

The scholarly aim of the book is to provide a few more pieces in the as yet incomplete picture of the role of women in the early church. These pieces are necessary if we are to see the whole portrait correctly. The practical aim of the book is to draw the modern church's attention to the high regard in which the widows of the early church were held and to the material help they received. It is my hope that our consciousness will be raised about the elderly poor in our midst.

Many congregations in many denominations are upheld by their faithful widows. Are all of them provided for? Or has the modern church reversed the pattern of early Christianity and allowed the widows to support the church? With respect to the widows, the modern church has a great deal of practical import to learn from its beginnings. This study is intended to provide a step in that direction.

1

The Widows

WHAT IS A "WIDOW"?

In common English usage, a "widow" is a woman who has lost her husband by death, has not remarried, and has thereby acquired certain legal rights of inheritance (from her husband's estate, for example). Although her emotional loss may be considerable, we do not usually regard the widow as legally defenseless or socially demoted because of her loss. In the ancient world, widows were not so fortunate legally and socially.

The Hebrew word for "widow"—*almanah*—has as its root the word *alem*, "unable to speak."[1] (It is related to an Aramaic word meaning to be in pain.) Thus, the widow was the "silent one." *Almanah* was used especially to refer to the widow as helpless or exposed to oppression and harsh treatment.[2] "Widowhood," *almenuth*, meant "silence,"[3] and the term expressed in poetic form exactly the legal status of the widow: she was not spoken for.

The Greek word for widow (*chēra*) comes from the Indo-European root *ghē*, which means "forsaken" or "left empty."[4] (The English word "widow" is also descended from this root.)[5] *Chēra* is related to the preposition *chōris*, "without" or "apart from," and is used adverbially to mean "separately" or "by itself" (see, for example, John 20:7). It is also related to the noun *chōra*, "region" or "empty space." The original meaning is a person "without" or "left without."[6] In the New Testament the term signifies a woman left without a husband. Hence, *chēra* can mean not only a widow in the modern sense of the word, but also a "woman living without a husband."[7] Henri Leclercq suggests that it signifies "anyone destitute, miserable; anyone who lived in solitude."[8] It has also been suggested that *chēra* simply designates a celibate woman.[9]

"Widow" frequently connoted not only marital but also economic status. A widow was often "left without" money or financial support as well as (or as a result of being) "left without" a husband. "The term *chēra* has a strong social and financial overtone more appropriate to a widow than a widower. Thus the more passive and needy status of women meant that a Greek woman who was left without a spouse was left a 'widow,' a 'person without a source of support.' "[10] This was almost uniformly the case in the ancient world.

By the first century A.D., the Greek term *monandros* is infrequently encountered as a term for a woman married only once.[11] The Latin *vidua* was the more common term for a widow, although *univira* was used as a term of approbation for widows who did not remarry after the death of their first husbands.

Hereafter, unless it is specifically noted that we are referring to the more general sense of a woman living without a husband or to a woman in some other circumstance, "widow" will denote a woman who has not remarried after the death of her husband.

WIDOWS IN THE ANCIENT WORLD

From a legal standpoint, the position of widows in ancient societies varied widely from culture to culture, age to age, and, within the same historical period, from place to place. Generally speaking, the position of women rises the further west one goes in the ancient world. Thus, we can say that women in Athens generally had fewer legal rights than those in Egypt or Rome. But in order to understand clearly the social and legal position of the widow in the New Testament period, it is necessary to paint in broad strokes her portrait in three worlds: the Greek, the Hebrew, and the Roman.

Women and Widows in the Greek World

Although there are some Attic inscriptions which indicate that women participated in the trades and professions, few inscriptions show that women owned property.[12] In classical Athens women did not participate in public life but kept homes and raised legitimate children for the husband, the *kyrios* (lord) of the *oikos* (house). The educated women were the *hetaerae,* who provided intellectual conversation and recreational sex for men. (A marriage contract we have from 311 B.C. specifically restricts the use of such concubines, and the husband is to return his wife's dowry if he "cheats.")[13] Until the Antonine constitution of A.D. 212, a woman needed her father or husband to witness any public act.

Upon the death of her husband, the widow was subject to the executor of his estate. The widow might look after the husband's property only until an heir was established or the guardian of the children had taken charge. Widows could not inherit property from their husbands if there were children. There are records of husbands making arrangements on their deathbeds so that their wives would not be left widows.[14] (Recall that Odysseus tells Penelope to remarry if he has not returned by the time his son has a beard.)[15]

Although a young widow was expected to remarry, she could remain at her first husband's house and be maintained by the new *kyrios* or return to her own family with her dowry. Whatever man was *kyrios* of her dowry was required to maintain her.[16] It was the duty of the *kyrios* of a young widow to find her a husband, although the widow had some choice concerning her second husband. If marriage was not possible, the widow was entitled to maintenance on the interest from her dowry. If she did remarry, her property was separated from her late husband's. His property went to the children. "Widows on their remarriage received dowries in exactly the same way as unmarried girls, and this is only natural since a woman's dowry was deemed to be her share of her paternal estate, a share set apart for her maintenance."[17]

If an older widow did not remarry, she could return to her household and manage her own money, although her son's permission was required to obtain a loan. Since her age was thought to be protection against assault, she had more freedom of movement than younger widows. While the state made provision for looking after older women, and children were to insure that their elderly parents were looked after, at least one Aristophanic widow plaited myrtle wreaths for a living,[18] and there are records of widows who were midwives and messengers. If a widow were above the age of sixty, she could earn money as a professional mourner at funerals.[19]

Spartan women (who owned 40 percent of Sparta's real estate) held higher social positions than their Athenian sisters, and rural women were less restricted than urban women, but the general position of women did not improve greatly until the end of the fourth century B.C., when a new attitude toward "inferior" beings (animals, slaves, women, children) developed. As Hellenism spread under Alexander the Great (356–323), Greeks came into contact with courts in which there were strong queens. An improvement in the status of women in Hellenistic times can be linked to the princesses, queens, and strong mothers of oriental courts, and perhaps to the fact that women played a greater role in oriental cults than in Greco-Roman religions.[20]

Greek women living in the far-off reaches of the empire were given more liberty than they would have had at home. Athenian women who married men in the provinces were given special privileges to compensate for relocating in unfamiliar territory. Wives began to be addressed as *kyria* (lady) to match the *kyrios* (lord). There is evidence of women at public gatherings in Hellenistic times, and of women as professional athletes, singers, and physicians. Education for women became more available; in Hellenistic Egypt more women than men could sign their names.[21]

It has been observed that ancient Greek society was patriarchal and collective, like Hebrew society, while Hellenistic society was more individualistic.[22] This shift toward individualism accounts for the improved position of women generally, and of widows specifically, in Hellenistic times. To understand the shift's impact, however, it is necessary to review the position of widows in the Hebrew tradition.

Women and Widows in the Hebrew World

Although Joachim Jeremias deals with a later period, the picture he presents of the social position of women at the time of Jesus is instructive.[23] Under the Torah, women were inferior to men. Women were not bound by the Commandments. Schools were almost solely for boys. The worship area of the synagogue was open to women; the study area was not. A woman's religious rights were limited; she was forbidden to teach and had no right to bear witness.[24]

Unmarried women generally stayed at home, and women were to remain unobserved in public. Until age twelve anything a female child made or found belonged to her father. Up to age twelve and one-half the father could marry her to anyone or sell her into slavery; after that she could not be betrothed against her will.

Twelve to twelve and one-half was the normal age of betrothal and transfer of power over a female from father to husband. Betrothal signified the acquisition of the woman by the man. Couples were married one year after betrothal, and normally went to live with the husband's family. The husband's job was to provide for the wife; the wife's duties were in the household. In a servile position to her husband, the wife was to obey the husband as master. Polygamy was permissible, and a wife had to tolerate living with concubines (although this was apparently uncommon because it was too expensive). The right to divorce was exclusively the husband's, and in the event of divorce children remained with the father.

Nevertheless, even early in the Hebrew tradition "to remain unmarried or to have no offspring was a bitter misfortune."[25] Furthermore, to be a widow was the fate most feared and bewailed by women. A husband's death before old age was considered a retribution for his sins, and this retribution was apparently incurred also by the wife. Therefore, to be left a widow was a disgrace.[26] When Naomi, Ruth's mother-in-law, comes to Bethlehem she laments, "Do not call me Naomi [pleasant], call me Mara [bitter], for the Almighty has dealt very bitterly with me. . . . The Lord has afflicted me and the Almighty has brought calamity upon me" (Ruth 1:20-21). In a song of assurance to Israel, the prophet Isaiah promises, "The reproach of your widowhood you will remember no more" (Isa. 54:4).

After her husband's death, a widow could return to her family only if her purchase price was repaid to her husband's heirs. Otherwise, she was forced to remain in a low position in his family. She could be sold into slavery for debt. Remarriage was not forbidden, but it was frowned upon.[27] The widow was expected to wait for levirate marriage (marriage to a brother of her husband in order to ensure male heirs in his line) or a public refusal of her before she could remarry outside her husband's family (see Deut. 25:5-10). Remarriage is mentioned only four times in the Old Testament,[28] and there are only two recorded instances of it outside the levirate tradition.[29]

As Gustav Stählin notes, "The main plight of widows was in the legal sphere."[30] In contrast to the Babylonian, Hittite, and Assyrian codes of law, the Hebrew code made no provision for the widow, except in the case of levirate marriage. In every other code, the widow had rights of inheritance, "but in Hebrew legislation she is passed over completely."[31] In the Old Testament, the widow's lot was so unhappy and piteous that undue severity against her was prohibited and, along with strangers, orphans, and the poor, she was commended to the charity of the people.

The protection of widows, orphans, and the poor did not begin with the Old Testament; it was common policy of the ancient Near East. The protection of widows, orphans, and the poor was the will of the gods, the virtue of kings, and the duty of common people in ancient Mesopotamia, Egypt, and Ugarit. "These people [widows, orphans, the poor] had no rights, no legal personalities, or in some cases possibly restricted rights. They were almost outlaws. Anyone could oppress them without danger that legal connections might endanger his position. To restore the balance of society these people must be protected."[32] In the Old Testament, God is viewed as the only one who can ultimately bring justice and deliverance to the weak, but in the Covenant Code (cf. Exod. 22:21-24; 23:6; Deut. 10:18; 14:28-29) the vertical line to God is clearly linked with the horizontal line of response to the poor.[33]

In the Law, the Prophets, and the wisdom literature of the Old Testament, God is the protector of the legally defenseless; God will "hear their cry" (Exod. 22:23; cf. Deut. 10:18; Ps. 146:9) and punish those who oppress them (Exod. 22:24; Deut. 27:19; Mal. 3:5; Ps. 94:6). God is the "protector of widows" (Ps. 68:5); God "tears down the house of the proud, but maintains the widow's boundaries" (Prov. 15:25).

The prohibitions against oppression of widows and the provisions for their assistance are specific: every three years the widow is to receive a portion of the tithe of produce (Deut. 14:28-29); her garment is not to be taken in pledge (Deut. 24:17-18);[34] she is to be invited to meals at public festivals (Deut. 16:11,14); and she is allowed to glean in the vineyards and fields (Deut. 24:19-24; cf. Ruth). Since the widow apparently wore special clothing (Gen. 38:14,19), ignorance was no excuse in the matter of protection of widows. On several occasions, Job cites his treatment of widows as an example of his goodness (Job 29:13; 31:16). The prophets upheld the cause of the widows,[35] and their prophecies that God will act in the day of judgment against those who mistreat widows prove that widows were indeed harshly treated.[36]

As noted earlier, the Hebrew word for "widow" closely resembles the word for "unable to speak." The widows were, symbolically at least, those without legal power of speech in the Hebrew tradition. In *Women in Judaism,* Leonard Swidler concludes that the status of women in Hebrew society was severely inferior to that of men, and that this inferiority broadened from the return from exile to talmudic times.[37] Widows held the lowest position among women. Coming from a Hebrew background, Jesus of Nazareth had an unprecedented attitude toward women and the plight of widows. Before we examine that attitude, however, one more color must be added to our picture of widows in the ancient world.

Women and Widows in the Roman Empire

Generally speaking, the legal status of women improved dramatically as the Roman Empire carried forward the liberating trends of Hellenistic Greece.[38] In the late Roman Republic, women could marry and divorce and could give evidence as legal witnesses. Under the empire, women ran for office in Pompeii, were sent on imperial missions to proconsuls, and led full economic and social lives. Legal equality in marriage reached almost "modern" standards. From a legal standpoint, divorce was equally easy for wife and husband. Even if a woman took the initiative in divorce proceedings, she could retain her dowry (if not her children, who apparently always remained with the father).[39]

Greek marriage contracts from Egypt offer the fullest evidence on marriage contracts in the Hellenistic-Roman world. There, the husband's duties are to maintain his wife in a suitable manner for a free woman. He is not to bring another woman into the *oikos* or *domus* (house) or to beget by one, nor is he to mistreat his wife. The development of such contracts in Egypt indicates a less patriarchal power structure and higher social and legal status for women.[40] We must be cautious, however, with evidence from Egypt since Greco-Roman practice was no doubt influenced by the more liberal tendencies mentioned above.

Roman women had more freedom than Athenian or Hebrew women. They were able to own and manage property and, thus, to accumulate wealth. By the time of Juvenal, privileged Roman women were educated.[41] In the eastern provinces they discharged liturgies and held magistracies, although it is debatable whether or not these were honorary posts.[42]

Social tensions related to the household in the later Roman period seem to have centered around the growing influence of women in society.[43] Members of the Roman ruling class viewed the "traditional, patriarchal family as a positive force in maintaining the stability of the political order,"[44] and departures from it were considered subversive, to the degree that role reversals in grooming and dress were condemned (see 1 Cor. 11:14-15). When we discuss the role of the widows in the early Christian community, it will be important to recall that the traditional household and conventional sex roles "had come to be associated on a symbolic level with the preservation of an orderly and stable society. Consequently, people whose behavior defied the traditional values in this area risked the charge of political subversion."[45]

From the eighth century B.C. to Christian Rome, a *univira* (*univiria*) was a woman who married only once.[46] At first, the designation's descriptive uses were associated with a social elite, but it later referred to other social classes and became a pagan epithet for a good wife. (Its use on small tombstones with short inscriptions indicates persons of moderate means.) While divorce was rare in the early republic, by the first century B.C. it was common (only Christians undertook lifelong fidelity and attempted to prohibit widows from remarrying),[47] and *univira* became a term of approbation for a once-married woman who died before her husband.[48]

A man who died before his wife could leave her a legacy so long as it was not greater than that left to his heirs. There is evidence that widows commissioned tombstones and inscriptions for their husbands.[49] Although twice-married women were less socially esteemed (and in an ideal society no woman married more than once), widows were encouraged by the state to remarry. Unless a widow were over fifty years of age, she was given twelve months to find a new husband. Widows who did not were debarred from inheritance from the first marriage. Augustus was apparently more concerned with propagation than with even waiting long enough to see if the widow were pregnant by the first husband. A widow from twenty to fifty years of age was to marry within one year of her husband's death or suffer considerable material disadvantage.[50]

Much later in Rome's history, laws that forced women to remarry were relinquished by Christian rulers who understood second marriages as impropriety. Second marriages were discouraged in favor of a chaste life, and the church, as we shall see, gave widows a code of behavior and social legitimacy.[51] From being used to praise a woman who married once, *monandros* and *univira* came to praise chastity for the love of God.[52]

CONCLUSIONS

Throughout the ancient world, except in Egypt, the legal position of women was uniformly low. Women's legal status was always inferior to that of men, and widows had fewer legal rights than married women. With limited rights of inheritance from her husband, a Roman widow was better off, at least in theory, than Greek and Hebrew widows, who were dependent upon the charity of the family or the state. In classical Greece, a woman's dowry was used to support her in the event of her husband's death. A Hebrew widow, if not protected by *ketubah* (a marriage contract containing, among other things, a settlement on the wife of a certain amount payable at her husband's death), could sue to recover a portion of her dowry.[53] Roman widows could function legally as independent parties if their financial circumstances allowed. We can speculate that the Jews of the Hellenistic-Roman Diaspora must have been influenced by their pagan neighbors in the matter of women's legal rights. But the legal literature from the Hebrew tradition puts widows at the very bottom of the social scale.

We have here sketched a portrait of the widow in the ancient world prior to the time of Jesus. In contrast to this bleak portrayal, the place of widows in Christian society from the late first century onward is much improved. Indeed, the widow even becomes an exemplary figure. The reasons for the dramatic change will be evident from our discussion of widows in the New Testament.

2

Widows in the New Testament

In contrast to Greco-Roman culture, the New Testament writers[1] manifest a relatively open attitude toward women. While the New Testament evidence is not sufficient to suggest full equality, "the prominence given to women is an unusual feature of social movements of the early empire,"[2] and certainly the Christian movement challenged suspicion toward women in the religions of the time. This is particularly significant since "women were the mainstay of religion in the ancient world."[3]

We must not, however, overestimate the extent to which Christianity improved the lot of women. The position of women in the early church was determined by the restrictions of the various societies through which Christianity spread.[4] Many scholars now note that society's inhibiting cultural demands and taboos have been misinterpreted as theological decisions on the part of the church. The literary records show a radical change in the status of women in Christianity from the early apostolic period (c. A.D. 50) to the beginning of the second century. Women seem to have exerted more influence at earlier stages, and to have been increasingly restricted as time went on. The principal explanations for this phenomenon are (1) that the character of ministry in the church was changing, (2) that the canon of Scripture was still in dispute, and (3) that the delay of the Parousia (the second coming of Christ) led the church to adapt to the social conditions in which it found itself. Because these three issues lie behind the New Testament texts—and behind the development of religious orders in the church—it is useful to summarize each briefly before turning to the texts themselves.

1. In the earliest Christian communities there was no particularized office of ministry. The New Testament "knows of no cultic Christian priesthood, no clearly designated office of sacerdotal responsibilities."[5] In other words, the ministry was determined "not by status

conferred but by function fulfilled."[6] Leadership was charismatic, rooted in the experience of and obedience to the Spirit. To use Pauline terminology, different persons had different gifts, and these gifts were used to build up the church. This participatory structure was gradually replaced by patriarchal office and cultic ministry.[7] The divergence of opinion about the extent of women's ministry in the early church is due in part to the diversity of practice in the various New Testament communities,[8] but it seems clear that as ministry changed from a function (exercising a gift) to an office, women were increasingly excluded.

2. The New Testament canon was in flux until the fourth century. Before the canon was settled upon, different groups appealed to different books as authoritative. This contributed to the wide variety of attitudes toward and opportunities for women in the churches. (For an example of recent scholarship on this matter, see the work of Elaine Pagels on the gnostic gospels.)[9] For our purpose the noteworthy point is that the writings of the early church were shaped by a struggle involving a variety of groups over, among other issues, the equality of women. The Scriptures "cannot be taken as a complete history of the actual condition of women in the early church."[10]

3. Finally, and perhaps most crucially for all aspects of the study of the early church and its literature, the Parousia did not come as expected. The radical statement of Paul in Gal. 3:28 that in Christ there is "neither Jew nor Greek, . . . slave nor free, . . . male nor female" represents an ethics for the interim before the return of Christ in which artificial religious, social, and sexual laws no longer hold. "All people now live under the same expectancy and the same promise for the future."[11] In light of the urgency of the end times, a new and more equal role for men and women in Christ was forged.

But the end time did not come, and the church was called upon to deal with questions of orthodoxy and organization. Furthermore, the church was forced to face what those outside the Christian community thought of it. As the church began to conform to the society around it, some of its original social radicalism was lost.[12] When the later church lost the vision that the kingdom was coming, it "also lost the theology that enabled it to live as though the Kingdom were at hand."[13] The church began to give two divergent messages: equality in Christ and the practice of subordination of women. To put the matter simply, "the heresy problem combined with social pressure and caused the church to move from a *communitas* structure challenging society's norms to a patriarchal structure embracing them."[14]

When we turn to the New Testament texts, the changing status of women and, in particular, widows is evident when we survey the material in roughly chronological order. It is important to recall that early Christianity inherited many of its attitudes toward widows from the Hebrew Bible and the Septuagint (the Greek translation of the Hebrew). As we have noted, the widow stands with the stranger, the orphan, and the poor as a special object of God's concern. Persons were admonished to treat these unfortunates well because God was their special helper and refuge. In short, "the Hebraic widow was an image of that poor, desolate 'remnant' of Israel destined to receive the promise."[15] The widow's spiritual task was to wait and pray for fulfillment. Anna (Luke 2:36-37) is, as we shall see, the paradigm for this activity and for the role of widows in general in the church's earliest period. To survey the New Testament chronologically, however, we must begin with the genuine Pauline epistles.

PAUL

When Paul mentions widows (1 Cor. 7:8, 39-40; Rom. 7:3), he does so peripherally in the course of answering questions concerning marriage and the law. In 1 Corinthians, Paul refers to widows in a discussion of remarriage. While Paul does not recommend remarriage, he leaves the decision to those concerned—"the unmarried and the widows." ("But if they cannot exercise self-control, they should marry" [1 Cor. 7:9]. "She is free to be married. . . . But in my judgment she is happier if she remains as she is" [7:39-40].)

While I agree with Stählin that Paul understands it as a *charisma* to remain unmarried,[16] since self-control is emphasized, Paul may be concerned with, among other things, how outsiders view the Christian community. Perhaps Paul's admonitions are directed at young Christians in the city of Corinth, a city not known for sexual restraint!

Mary McKenna suggests that, because Paul composed 1 Corinthians in Ephesus, he must have noted the relative freedom of the women in that pluralistic community. Since Paul lived in Corinth for a year and a half, he would have known that the Jewish Christian women there had no rights in the synagogue and that they sat silent in a separate area. McKenna suggests that Paul may be associating freedom and widowhood, knowing that relative freedom would appeal to women in the Hellenic world.[17] While this is an ingenious thesis and it certainly makes Paul a more appealing character than he sometimes appears in relation to women, it does not square with the general intent of 1 Cor. 7:8, 39-40. The status of widows is simply one aspect of the question Paul has apparently been asked about marriage: "Now concerning the matters about which you wrote . . ." (7:1). And the marriage question itself falls under the general heading of Paul's concern about reports of immorality in the Corinthian congregation (cf. 5:1-5; 6:9-20; 7). Since 1 Corinthians also addresses the issue of women's head covering (11:2-16) and silence in the church (14:33b-36), it is more likely that we are dealing with the breakdown of a congregation that is beginning to be infiltrated by gnostic elements.[18]

In Romans, Paul mentions widows in the context of a discussion of law. He argues that law is binding only until death (Rom. 7:1), and he uses the analogy of marriage to demonstrate that "one who has died to sin is no more bound to it than is a woman to her deceased husband."[19] The passage does not shed any light on Paul's view of widows or on the widow's role in the Christian community.

At this point, all that we can safely conclude about Paul's understanding of widows is that they are, in his judgment, happier (*makariotera*, from *makarios*, literally, "blessed" or "fortunate")[20] if they remain widows. Paul's reasons for this statement must be deduced from what other New Testament texts, and extracanonical sources, tell us about the position of widows in the Christian community.

JESUS

Widows play a significant role in only two of the Synoptic Gospel traditions: in Mark, and in the special Lukan material.[21] Jesus' mention of widows in Mark is largely for symbolic purposes. Outside the pastoral epistles, there is more material on the widows in Luke-Acts than anywhere else in the New Testament.

Markan Tradition

Mark uses Jesus' reference to widows in 12:38-44 to show how Jesus "stepped forward as the true advocate of the oppressed and

exploited."[22] The first reference is part of a general warning against
the scribes, who exhibit ostentation and unhealthy craving for position (Mark 12:38-40).[23] Specifically, they "devour widows' houses"
(v. 40).[24] The seizure of widows' houses "would be under the forms
of civil law, but in contravention of the Divine law of love."[25] Jesus
is warning the people against religious leaders who hide their lack
of compassion under a show of piety. Since widows are without legal
recourse, mistreatment of them is especially ugly.

Mark closes the scene in the temple with the story of the widow's
mite:

> And [Jesus] sat down opposite the treasury, and watched the multitude
> putting money into the treasury. Many rich people put in large sums.
> And a poor widow came, and put in two copper coins, which make a
> penny. And he called his disciples to him, and said to them, "Truly, I
> say to you, this poor widow has put in more than all those who are
> contributing to the treasury. For they all contributed out of their abun-
> dance; but she out of her poverty has put in everything she had, her
> whole living." (Mark 12:41-44; cf. Luke 21:1-4)

The point of the passage is not the status of the widow but "the
contrast between the outward meagreness and inward richness of the
widow's service, and the outward ostentation and inward barrenness
of the Pharisees' religion."[26] In comparison to those who have more
than enough and do not touch their capital to give alms, the widow,
who has little, puts in "her whole living" (literally, "her whole life").

Presumably, Jesus recognizes the widow from her clothing.[27] As is
frequently the case when Jesus demonstrates the nature of the kingdom, he upsets the normal pattern of worldly values. "Money values
are not the standard of gifts in the kingdom of God."[28] She who had
given least had given most. The widow becomes a symbol of unselfish
generosity and trust; her total giving "presupposes total trust in God
and His provision."[29] What she symbolizes in this pericope will be
reflected in what she is called upon to do as the order of widows
develops. At this point we simply note that Jesus knows the unfor-
tunate position of widows. Jesus' divine wisdom and compassion are
depicted by Mark in the reaction to and elevation of a particularly
generous widow.[30]

Lukan Tradition

The Lukan tradition adds to the Markan tradition three more passages on Jesus and widows. In one, Jesus intervenes directly to help a particular widow (Luke 7:11-15); in the other two, the widows are used illustratively (4:25-26; 18:1-8). Luke also provides us with a picture of the prototypical pre-Christian widow—Anna (2:36-38). Then, in Acts, we encounter our first specific information about the order of widows and some of its first members.

Luke's interest in the widows reflects his general concern for the poor and oppressed, especially women. As we look at the amount of material Luke provides on women, it is clear that Alfred Plummer is correct in calling it the Gospel of womanhood.[31] "Nearly one-third of the material unique to Luke deals directly with women."[32] It has been noted that Luke's Hellenistic background helps to account for his Gospel's more emancipated attitude toward women. The Gospel was apparently shaped in a social context in which large numbers of women were present.[33] It has even been suggested that Mary, the mother of Jesus, was the source for some of the evangelist's insights in the infancy narratives.[34]

We encounter in Anna (Luke 2:36-38) a figure who serves as an example for the later order of Christian widows and who, with Simeon (and like Zechariah and Elizabeth in chap. 1), provides us with an example of Luke's practice of pairing male and female stories. In Lukan material we find pairings of characters—a story dealing with a man and then a similar story dealing with a woman.[35] After completing his report of Simeon's blessing of Jesus, Luke gives us a female counterpart in Anna:

> And there was a prophetess, Anna, the daughter of Phanuel, of the tribe of Asher; she was of a great age, having lived with her husband seven years from her virginity, and as a widow till she was eighty-four. She did not depart from the temple, worshiping with fasting and prayer night and day. And coming up at that very hour she gave thanks to God, and spoke of him to all who were looking for the redemption of Jerusalem (Luke 2:36-38).

Anna's authenticity as a historical character is attested by the fact that she is not given a hymn. Friedrich Schleiermacher, arguing against the interpretation that this narrative is purely poetical, asks,

"Why should the author . . . have introduced Anna, who is not made even to answer any poetical purpose?"[36]

We might first note that there is evidence from Qumran of a female order for the aged. The theme of longevity is present in the 344 fragments of 4Q502 (first century B.C.). A joyous occasion that gives special prominence to elderly men and women is described. In arguing that the fragments do not describe a marriage ritual, Joseph Baumgarten mentions "ancient virgins" who avoided marriage and children because of "their ardent yearning for wisdom." He notes that there were women in the community at Qumran who never married and who dwelt in camps.[37] They were the blessed, undefiled women described in the Wisdom of Solomon who have "not entered into a sinful union" and who "will have fruit when God examines souls" (Wisd. 3:13). Baumgarten suggests that 4Q502 deals with this female order.

Luke tells us of Anna's great age (sixty years of age was considered elderly).[38] Some commentators have suggested that Luke 2:36 means that Anna remained a virgin even after she married. Although no connection can be established between Anna and the "ancient virgins" of Qumran, she certainly exhibits many of the characteristics of that group. At the very least we can say there was precedent in the Jewish world of the time for consecrated elderly women.

In the context of the widows, the answer to Schleiermacher's question has to do with the motifs Anna introduces. One is asceticism. She has had a relatively short marriage, but has continued as a widow for over eighty years. In Luke 2:37 the word "till" draws attention to the length of her widowhood. Her abstinence from a second marriage is reflected in later Christian teaching (cf. 1 Cor. 7:8-9, 39-40; 1 Tim. 3:9-16) and, in fact, it was soon held to be honorable, indeed exemplary, not to remarry. Tertullian later wrote, "Monogamy is a custom of the highest honor."[39]

Anna's asceticism, which was later required of "enrolled" widows, also included fasting and prayer: "In spite of her age she kept more than the customary fasts, . . . perhaps more than the Mondays and Thursdays, . . . and spent an unusual amount of time in prayer."[40] Like widows and tears, widows and prayer are often related in the New Testament.[41] The combination of fasting and prayer soon became crucial to the spiritual work of the early Christian community (cf.

Acts 13:1-3); and Anna's presence in the temple became a model for
the first community of disciples (cf. Luke 24:53; Acts 2:46).[42]

In addition to providing the prototype for what later became the
"consecrated widows" and for the early Christian community in general, Anna is introduced by Luke as a prophetess (*prophētis*). From a
historic tribe or family (see Josh. 19:24-31), Anna is in the tradition
of Miriam, Deborah, and Huldah, and she foreshadows the honorable
Christian calling of prophet held by, among others, the daughters of
Philip (Acts 21:9): "Anna was a woman divinely inspired to make
known God's will to others."[43] Her role as prophetess makes her an
unusually credible witness as she speaks of Jesus "to all who were
looking for the redemption of Jerusalem" (Luke 2:38). Luke at the
end of the Gospel gives women the task of proclaiming Jesus' resurrection (Luke 24:8-10); here at the beginning a woman proclaims
Jesus' advent. Anna is the first evangelist.

Since we have already discussed the implications of the episode of
the widow's mite for our study, we shall not repeat Luke's version
of it in 21:1-4. Instead, we turn to the other widow Luke mentions
who was a historical person, the widow of Náin (7:11-17). Since
Luke is often the only evangelist to give us material about women,
the fact that he alone records the event should not be sufficient to
call into question its historical character.

The loss of a child is always devastating for a parent, but the con-
struction of Luke 7:12 indicates why Jesus would have special
compassion[44] for this woman. The dead man was her only son (*mon-
ogenēs*). He therefore represented her main claim to status in the community. (Daughters, if she had them, were something of a liability.)
To make matters worse: ". . . and she was a widow [*chēra*]." Luke's
choice of the coordinate conjunction "and" has the effect of height-
ening her loss; she is now without a legal protector. In short, her
"social security" is gone. When Jesus raises this man from the dead,
he is in fact restoring two persons to life in the community: the man
and his mother.

It has been suggested that this account rests heavily upon the story
of Elijah's raising the only son of the widow in 1 Kgs. 17:17-24. It
is characteristic of Luke to treat Jesus as a new Elijah; in fact, this
story may well have been, in Luke's mind, "an amplification of Jesus'
reference in his synagogue sermon at Nazareth (4:26) to Elijah's visit

to the widow."[45] The phrase "gave him to his mother" (Luke 7:15) echoes 1 Kgs. 17:23; this parallelism between Luke and 1 Kings and the crowd's response, "a great prophet has risen among us" (Luke 7:16), is hard to ignore. Furthermore, the figure of the weeping mother in the story may suggest Mother Israel. "Jesus is the one who restores to her her lost children."[46] In light of the many symbolic uses of the figure of the widow in the Old Testament, this reading is likely to be correct. And it would be consistent with Luke's Jesus, who refers to the widow and Elijah (4:25-27) and who makes symbolic use of the widow in the parable of the unjust judge.

In his teaching in the synagogue at Nazareth (Luke 4:16-30), Jesus expounds texts from Isaiah. He asserts that a prophet is not acceptable in his own country, and uses 1 Kgs. 17:17-24 as an illustration. Jesus refers to the widow in Zarephath (1 Kgs. 17:18-24) to demonstrate how God releases God's messengers from human ties, especially ties to one's own people, one's racial or national group.[47] Gentiles sometimes receive God's help when Israel does not. Thus, the widow once again appears in connection with a major Lukan theme: the universality of the gospel, specifically, the extension of its message beyond its Jewish origins.

Jesus' final illustrative use of the widow occurs in the parable of the unjust judge:

> And he told them a parable, to the effect that they ought always to pray and not lose heart. He said, "In a certain city there was a judge who neither feared God nor regarded man; and there was a widow in that city who kept coming to him and saying, 'Vindicate me against my adversary.' For a while he refused; but afterward he said to himself, 'Though I neither fear God nor regard man, yet because this widow bothers me, I will vindicate her, or she will wear me out by her continual coming.' " And the Lord said, "Hear what the unrighteous judge says. And will not God vindicate his elect, who cry to him day and night? Will he delay long over them? I tell you, he will vindicate them speedily. Nevertheless, when the Son of man comes, will he find faith on earth?" (Luke 18:1-8)

Luke positions the parable after Jesus' remarks on the end of the age (17:22-37) and before the parable of the Pharisee and the tax collector (18:9-14), which again warns against outward displays of piety not accompanied by inward commitment. It is a familiar context for the appearance of a widow.

Interestingly, Luke has Jesus begin by carefully stating the point of the parable to his disciples: "They ought always to pray and not lose heart" (Luke 18:1). The issue between the judge and the woman is financial: she is a widow seeking vindication. "Typical of defenselessness: she had neither protector to coerce, nor money to bribe the unrighteous magistrate."[48] Without an opponent in view, the judge is unwilling to decide for the widow.[49]

Plummer suggests that we are to understand the judge to be a gentile official with no respect for either the *vox Dei* or the *vox populi.* The judge consciously defies both divine commands and public opinion:[50] "I neither fear God nor regard man" (Luke 18:4). He does, however, finally respond to the persistent widow lest she wear him out. The Greek for "to wear out" is derived from a word meaning "to give a black eye," "to beat black and blue," "to annoy greatly." In short, the judge fears continual annoyance more than he fears a single assault.

The point of the parable is, of course, that God will "vindicate his elect, who cry to him day and night" (18:7). Prayer, even if it appears to be ignored, will be answered; it is not turned aside or silenced by anything. Even the least powerful member of the community can gain access, indeed, is assured access, to the kingdom.[51] The question is, Why choose the figure of a widow, beyond its suggestion of powerlessness? Why not a beggar or a child?

Stählin has argued that we must not look at this story alone but as part of a cycle of stories.[52] The stories show us that the widow was a collective type or character for the early Christian audience. Stählin notes how ancient cities or states took on women as their emblems. Christianity took such representations from pagan art and from Old Testament allegories: Jerusalem the "woman," the "daughter" of Zion, and "Mother" Israel. In modern literary terms, the widow in Luke 18 is a personification of the church in its time of struggle.[53] As a widow, the church in Luke's time is experiencing its forty years in the desert. Prayer is its only weapon in this struggle, and God will surely hear its prayers.[54] God's favorable hearing of prayer is the widow's—and the church's—certainty or assurance; when the end time comes, the Messiah will restore the widow. Stählin's reading of Luke 18:1-8 draws together a number of Lukan motifs we have noted in the passages on widows. It stresses the widow who prayed night and day (2:37), and who was prototypical of a later development. And it corroborates the echoes in 7:11-17 of Mother Israel and the restoration of her children. As in the example used by Jesus in his synagogue teaching (4:16-30), deliverance is granted to an unlikely candidate. Also evident is the reversal of human values which heralds the kingdom of God: the entreaties of the powerless effect deliverance. In the terms of the widow's mite, the least means the most.

In the ministry and teaching of Jesus, the widow appears as one of many examples of a new system of values breaking into the world. The widow's position and piety are no more to be lamented; she becomes exemplary. She is elevated to a position of spiritual prominence in the Christian order of things. In the figure of the widow we see a shining example of how God "has put down the mighty from their thrones, and exalted those of low degree" (Luke 1:52). This new status is reflected in the Acts of the Apostles, which gives us our clearest picture of the position of widows in the early church.

ACTS

As we have noted, the writings of the early church were shaped in part by a struggle among opposing groups over the equality of women and therefore cannot be taken as an objective record of the actual condition of women in the early church.[55] But even though the Acts of the Apostles is not objective and was written later, it is certainly a good source for studying the role women played in the spread of the church. Acts stresses Christianity among women, in part because the new faith had startling missionary success with women and slaves, who were receptive to a message of spiritual, if not literal, liberation. The women described in Acts were living under Roman law, the influence of which was felt even by Jewish women. While the Gospels originate predominantly in the rural, Jewish environment of Palestine, "Acts reflects contact with the urban (commercial) environment of the Hellenistic cities."[56]

Surveying Acts, we find at least twelve women mentioned by name.[57] These women were single, married, professionals (working outside the home), homemakers, Jews, Greeks, goddesses, Romans, sisters, mothers, mothers-in-law, prophetesses, missionaries, teachers, queens, slaves, and martyrs. In short, they reflect the whole spectrum of ancient society. Luke stresses that both men and women followed Jesus,[58] and that on Paul's missionary journeys, "women of standing" were especially receptive to his message (Acts 17:4, 12). Without consulting the list of Paul's co-workers in Romans 16, we find in Acts at least four women engaged in what we would now describe as church-related vocations,[59] and that list would not include women who founded house churches or who were probably part of early missionary couples.

Acts provides us with two examples of the care of widows in the Christian community (6:1-7; 9:36-43) and with a number of hints about the function and status of what was emerging as their "order." The first mention of the widows occurs in Acts 6:1-7:

> Now in these days when the disciples were increasing in number, the Hellenists murmured against the Hebrews because their widows were neglected in the daily distribution. And the twelve summoned the body of the disciples and said, "It is not right that we should give up preaching the word of God to serve tables. Therefore, brethren, pick out from among you seven men of good repute, full of the Spirit and of wisdom, whom we may appoint to this duty. But we will devote ourselves to prayer and to the ministry of the word." And what they said pleased the whole multitude, and they chose Stephen, a man full of faith and of the Holy Spirit, and Philip, and Prochorus, and Nicanor, and Timon, and Parmenas, and Nicolaus, a proselyte of Antioch. These they set before the apostles, and they prayed and laid their hands upon them.
>
> And the word of God increased; and the number of the disciples multiplied greatly in Jerusalem, and a great many of the priests were obedient to the faith.

The theological and ecclesiological interest in this passage has usually focused on the function of "the seven" or on the question raised by Acts 4:32-37 about the community of goods in the early church.[60] While the passage is very suggestive in terms of the organizational development of the church, that is not our primary interest. It should be noted that there was a history of public support of the poor among Jews. In Jerusalem at least, alms were not given directly to widows, but were collected by temple officials and put into a basket. No one could make a claim on this *kuppah* who had as much as a week's supply of food at home.[61] As friction developed between the Jews and the followers of Jesus, so did discrimination in financial matters.[62] Widows who had been supported by the temple were cut off when they became Christians.[63] The increasing number of Christians meant there were more poor people to accommodate. This necessitated the organizational development reflected in this passage.

The Hellenists and Hebrews mentioned in Acts 6:1 were not, strictly speaking, Greeks and Jews. A Hellenist (*hellēnistēs*) is a Greek-speaking Jew; the word "Hellenist" is derived from the verb *hellēnizō*, meaning "to Graecize" in speech or custom. According to Foakes Jackson and Kirsopp Lake, "Hebrews," *hebraioi*, on the other hand, "seems to refer primarily to nationality, not speech."[64] Johannes Munck, however, says "Hebrew" was the old name for the Jews who had Aramaic as their mother tongue and Greek as a second language. The Hellenists, Munck suggests, were Jews (like Paul) who grew up in the Diaspora with Greek as their native tongue.[65]

McKenna argues, on the basis of Acts 4:34-35, that the Hellenic widows were not in need, and suggests the Hellenic diaconate was established for official ministry or service (*diakonia*) that "had developed around the Galilean women who had followed and served the Lord, his Apostles, and his Church. These women deserved special honor, as did the Twelve themselves."[66] As the church grew, it was weaned from its Judaic origins, and Hellenic widows joined the ecclesial institution of widows. Since the Aramaic-speaking Galilean women had served the Lord, it is not surprising that they were given preference in the daily distribution.[67]

Evidence for the existence of an order of widows at this early stage is conjectural at best. I agree with Jackson and Lake that there is no reason to go beyond the ordinary meaning of "widows" here. They note, however, "that this passage regards the widows as receiving regular support, and this implies some organization of their members."[68] The further development of the organization is evident in 1 Tim. 5:9-16.

Disagreement about the stage of development of the order does not, however, invalidate McKenna's perceptive analysis of the reason for the partiality of the distribution. If the Hebraic widows were among the women mentioned by Luke in 8:1-3, 23-49, then their special treatment would have been understandable. The fact that in Luke 8:2-3 no husband is mentioned for Mary Magdalene or Susanna, but that Joanna is identified as the "wife of Chuza, Herod's steward" (8:3) might well suggest that the former were widows. (Stählin suggests this may be true of Tabitha [Dorcas] in Acts 9:36.)[69]

The most conservative reading of Acts 6:1-7 would suggest that at this point the church in Jerusalem had merely organized philanthropic work in behalf of its widows as a natural outgrowth both of its Jewish roots and of the teaching and example of Jesus. The widows, if organized at all, were grouped on the basis of cultural background.

In Acts 9:36-43, however, two meanings of the term "widow" become apparent: "(i) all women who had lost their husbands; (ii) a selected number of the first class who were appointed to a definite position in the organization of the Church as part of the 'Clerus.' "[70] The raising of Tabitha in Acts 9:36-43 continues the narrative of Peter's missionary activity:

> Now there was at Joppa a disciple named Tabitha, which means Dorcas. She was full of good works and acts of charity. In those days she fell sick and died; and when they had washed her, they laid her in an upper room. Since Lydda was near Joppa, the disciples, hearing that Peter was there, sent two men to him entreating him, "Please come to us without delay." So Peter rose and went with them. And when he had come, they took him to the upper room. All the widows stood beside him weeping, and showing tunics and other garments which Dorcas made while she was with them. But Peter put them all outside and knelt down and prayed; then turning to the body he said, "Tabitha, rise." And she opened her eyes, and when she saw Peter she sat up. And he gave her his hand and lifted her up. Then calling the saints and widows he presented her alive. And it became known throughout all Joppa, and many believed in the Lord. And he stayed in Joppa for many days with one Simon, a tanner.

The peace alluded to in 9:31 gave Peter the opportunity to travel. As happened earlier, "wonders" accompanied the preaching of the Word and subsequent missionary advances.

The story of Tabitha is firmly in the Lukan tradition and exhibits one of his favorite themes: that the "works" done by Jesus are paralleled by "works" done by the postascension church. We should note, however, that this is the first time an apostle raises someone from the dead.

The passage is important for the study of the widows for two reasons. First, as in Acts 6:1-7, we see a group of widows who were apparently recipients of benevolence. Second, Tabitha acted in behalf of others. If Tabitha were a widow, as has been suggested, then she provides us with a link to the "order" in 1 Tim. 5:3-16.

Acts 9:39, 41 introduces a group of widows for whom Tabitha apparently had taken responsibility—she made clothing for them. Presumably it is these widows who had prepared Tabitha's body (v. 37). "It is possible that the widows came in the capacity, which they certainly had later in the Christian church, of nurses and professional mourners . . . but it seems more probably that they are present merely because they had benefited from the good deeds of Dorcas."[71] Jackson and Lake insist that the widows are recipients, not administrators, of charity. Although they are correct in asserting that "there is a real difference between Acts and the later ecclesiastical literature, beginning with the Pastoral Epistles,"[72] the text itself suggests that the widows were more than individuals who received clothing.

After Peter raises Tabitha, he calls the saints and widows (*tous hagious kai tas chēras*). The "saints" are clearly the assembled Christians; this is the standard usage in Paul's letters. The text gives no reason to suppose that widows were not members of the Christian community. We can therefore conjecture that Peter is calling the Christians, and a special group of Christians, the widows, to witness Tabitha's restoration. The friends of Tabitha may have belonged to a society. If so, we have evidence for a society of widows outside Jerusalem as early as A.D. 43.[73] Whether they had duties or were, like the widows in Acts 6:1-7, recipients of charity, cannot be determined with certainty.

Stählin suggests that Tabitha was herself a widow because no husband is mentioned. He feels that Tabitha cared for a group that was already a special class, and that her raising was, therefore, in the interest of the "order" of widows.[74] This reading has good company: "St. Basil interpreted Acts to mean that Tabitha was a widow in the ecclesial sense."[75] There are certainly examples both in pagan antiquity and in the Jewish community of generous women (2 Cor. 8:9 would provide the Christian motive for such generosity).[76] In Alexandria there is inscriptional evidence for the "women charged with the 'looking after' of the widows." Three papyri from Oxyrhynchos from the end of the fifth century speak of such women with a formula, "Widows of the holy (Christian) X."[77] This may shed light on what Luke meant by "saints and widows" in Acts 9:41. It is, however, dangerous to read backwards in historical studies. The collection of fragments speaks of what was, at least in the Egyptian church, an established system of care for and supervision of widows. Whether or not Tabitha was in such a relationship to the widows of Joppa (9:41-43) and was therefore a forerunner of later development must be left to the realm of speculation.

One final aspect of the text of Acts 9:36-43 must be examined before we draw some conclusions. In 9:36, Tabitha is introduced as a disciple: "At Joppa there was a disciple [*mathētria*] named Tabitha" (au. trans.). In its masculine form, *mathētēs* means "disciple," "pupil," or "follower." It is the word commonly used for the followers of Jesus, especially the Twelve. The feminine form, *mathētria*, occurs only once in the New Testament, here in 9:36, but there is no doubt about the accuracy of the text. Jackson and Lake suggest that it may occur only here because of the special use the author makes of *mathētēs* in chapter 9 (cf. vv. 1, 10, 19, 25, 26, 38).[78] There are at least two ways to view this. Acts uses the term "disciple," *mathētēs*, to denote members of the Christian religion, that is, "followers of Jesus." The term may denote nothing more in 9:36. There is, however, some doubt about whether "disciple" in the Gospels means the Twelve or a larger or smaller circle around Jesus.[79] The New Testament is not consistent about the number of disciples or who they are.[80] Elisabeth Schüssler Fiorenza discusses this point in her article "The Twelve." She notes the lack of consistency and explains that twelve is a symbolic number, not a historical or masculine number. For example, Mark speaks of "Twelve" and "disciples," but both are proved by suffering with Jesus as the faithful women also suffer with him.[81]

The feminine form *mathētria* is used in the apocryphal New Testament. In the *Gospel of Peter*, the term is used to apply to Mary Magdalene: "Now early on the Lord's day Mary Magdalene, a disciple (female) of the Lord, . . . (51) took with her the women her friends and (52) came into the tomb where he was laid."[82] In Coptic gnostic literature, "female disciples," *mathētriai*, corresponds to "male disciples," *mathētai*, which equals "apostles," *apostoloi*, and the group is headed, again, by Mary Magdalene.[83]

The most conservative reading of Acts 9:36 would be that Tabitha was simply a Christian, a follower of Jesus. In view of the imprecision of the term *mathētēs* in the New Testament, and the later use of *mathētria*, we can at least suggest the possibility that Tabitha was closer to Jesus. When summoned, Peter goes off to Joppa immediately

(9:38-39). Can he have known Tabitha from the group of "other women" who followed Jesus and ministered to him (Luke 8:1-3; 23:49; 24:10)? Like those women, Tabitha is "full of charity and good works" (9:36) and is apparently of independent means. Certainly Joppa was close enough to Jerusalem for Christians there to have maintained contact with the Jerusalem church in the early days after Jesus' ascension.

To summarize the incident at Joppa in which Peter raises Tabitha from the dead: Since no husband is mentioned it is possible that Tabitha was a widow, although, like her sisters in Luke 8:1-3, one with independent means. In its only appearance in the New Testament, *mathētria,* the feminine form of "disciple," is used to describe Tabitha. The widows mentioned collectively in 9:39, 41 may already have been a special class, since Peter calls them "saints and widows," suggesting that the widows were a recognizable group within the Christian community. Whether or not they were nurses and professional mourners, or simply recipients of charity, Tabitha had obviously taken special responsibility for them. Inscriptional evidence from Egypt (and, in fact, the life of Saint Pacomias's sister) indicates that women took on such duties. If this is the case in Acts, and if Tabitha were a widow, then she was actively engaged in work in behalf of the community and was not a passive recipient of its benevolence. She was practicing what James called "religion that is pure and undefiled before God" (James 1:27). And Tabitha's actions here were in accordance with Jesus' teaching that the Christian notion of "family" extends beyond blood relatives (Matt. 12:46-50). Tabitha fulfilled the later injunction in the pastoral epistles: "If any believing woman has relatives who are widows, let her assist them" (1 Tim. 5:16). In short, the case is reasonably strong for the existence of an "order" or "society" of widows outside Jerusalem at a very early stage in the church's development.

Furthermore, if, with Stählin, we assert that Tabitha was a widow since no husband is mentioned, and if we use the general definition of "widow" as a "woman living without a husband" or "anyone who lives in solitude," then we should have to include among the widows Mary the mother of John Mark (Acts 12:12); Lydia, Paul's first European convert (Acts 16:14);[84] Phoebe (Rom. 16:1); Mary in

Rom. 16:6; and Chloe in 1 Cor. 1:11. This would open up the possibility that widows served the early church as founders and sustainers of house churches, as deaconesses, and as assistants of Paul. All of these women would have to be included as forerunners of the congregation of widows to which we will turn our attention in 1 Tim. 5:3-16.

A brief treatment of the two final references to the widows in the New Testament will suffice since those passages do not significantly alter the picture that has already emerged. We have referred to James 1:27, which states that true religion is to "visit orphans and widows in their affliction." James deals with true religion that is more than devotional exercise. James echoes what we have heard from Jesus in Mark 12:38-44 and Luke 20:46-47, and continues the traditional teaching that caring for widows serves God (Hos. 6:6; Matt. 9:13; 25:40).

In Rev. 18:7 the widow is used figuratively in contrast to the harlot of Babylon. The harlot is haughty and mistakenly thinks she will never experience the humbling that befalls the widow. John uses "widow" as the extreme of lowliness and expects us to hear behind it the figurative use of the term in the Old Testament. In the Old Testament, when people are unfaithful they are widows in the sense of being abandoned ones.[85]

Both James and Revelation depict the widow in the low social and legal position she generally occupies in the ancient world. The bulk of the New Testament, however, reveals the possibility of a status for the widow, one that will include specific, constructive activities. As evidence of this we have discussed Anna (Luke 2:36-38), the ministering women of Luke 8:1-3, and the women in the Acts of the Apostles.

It is clear that by the late first century widows had an acknowledged claim to benevolence from and recognized status and privileges in the Christian community. When we examine the pastoral epistles, we find that the community, in turn, had expectations of and requirements for the widows that led to the establishment of an order. From this order came the most outstanding women in the first three centuries of the church.

3

Origins of
the Widows' Order

THE PASTORAL LETTERS IN GENERAL

An enormous amount of scholarly work has been done on the questions of the authorship, date, and purpose of the pastoral epistles—1 and 2 Timothy and Titus.[1] While it is not within the scope of this study to address these questions, their answers greatly affect the interpretation of specific passages in the letters. For our purposes, I assume (along with Martin Dibelius, Hans Conzelmann, Burton Scott Easton, Fred Gealy, A. J. B. Higgins, C. K. Barrett, and A. T. Hanson)[2] that the Pastorals are pseudonymous works, that is, written by someone else in Paul's name. Although it is possible that the author was a "secretary" of Paul's, it is doubtful that it was Luke (as suggested by C. F. D. Moule and others.)[3] Nor do the Pastorals represent a collection of Pauline fragments; the vocabulary, style, and theology of the letters seem to preclude this possibility.

While those who insist on Pauline authorship place the Pastorals as early as A.D. 57,[4] scholars who take them to be pseudonymous have suggested that they may have been written by 95 (just after Acts, of which the author apparently knew) or as late as 135 to 150. Most scholars place the writing of the Pastorals at the beginning of the second century, with a "likelihood of 100–105 being the correct date."[5] This allows for Polycarp's knowledge of the Pastorals[6] but places them before Ignatius of Antioch's letters, which exhibit persecution of the church that is not evident in the Pastorals. The internal evidence suggests that they were written from Asia Minor for Pauline churches of the same provenance.

Questions of origin and authorship aside, it is clear that the Pastorals depict the church as it moves from primitive simplicity to systems of doctrine and forms of government.[7] "In them we see the church as it sets out into the second century, tackling its practical problems."[8] Church order, false teaching, and social acceptability were the principal problems facing the church at that time.

The importance of church order is reflected in the attention the pastoral writer pays to the offices of ministry in the church.[9] Two types of ministry have been noted in the early church: charismatic (then current in the Pauline churches) and institutional (which later developed into early catholicism as expressed in the Pastorals). The idea that there was a strict division between the two types of ministry has today been abandoned in favor of the understanding that office and charism are not necessarily opposed to each other, and that different types of ministry coexisted in the churches of the New Testament period.[10] Still, "it is striking that Paul in his congregational letters points to the capacities and qualities of the leading persons and not to their official competence."[11] It is the pastoral writer who lists the qualifications for the offices of bishop (1 Tim. 3:1-7), deacon (3:8-13), widow (5:3-16), and elder (5:17-19).

While the pastoral writer presents these ministries from the disciplinary angle of a church order, and in conformity with this literary genre relies upon traditional material, especially from the Jewish community,[12] it is clear that the church has reached a turning point in its understanding of ministry. It is time for institutional rules and principles; "from the Pastorals onwards the ministry enters into a period of functionarization."[13] As Norbert Brox has noted, we see in the Pastorals the *Beruf* (calling) becoming an *Amt* (office).[14]

The centralizing trend in the authority of church offices was intended to strengthen the unity of congregations and to root out heresy. The letters of Saint Ignatius of Antioch (d. 115) also address these problems.[15] Leaders of the second-century church became aware of threats from within. They believed that the liberty Paul had allowed in the functions of ministry needed to be organized into recognized channels in order to prevent divisiveness and heresy. George Tavard has noted that the institution of widowhood was, along with other offices in the church, limited by this shift of policy.[16]

The struggle against heresy was a major reason for the development of the church's monepiscopal organization.[17] There is much speculation about the precise nature of the false teaching to which the pastoral writer alludes. If the letters are from the early second century (my position), then the author may have been facing a form of Gnosticism. The presence of Gnosticism in the early church has received much scholarly attention.[18] Two aspects of the gnostic presence are of specific concern for our understanding of the widows: first, the likelihood that women in particular were attracted to Gnosticism; and second, the way in which the author attacks these "heretics."

The problem of Gnosticism in the church was, of course, not sex-specific. Both men and women were in danger of wandering into "vain discussion" (1 Tim. 1:6), "godless and silly myths" (1 Tim. 4:7), "stupid controversies, genealogies, dissensions" (Titus 3:9). It has been noted, however, that asceticism had particular appeal for women, especially in the eastern provinces of the Roman Empire. An ascetic way of life, which featured chastity and the severing of family ties, had special impact on women. Well-to-do women who found their traditional domestic roles inadequate or socially marginal looked to ascetic Christianity for standards of worth more consonant with their circumstances.[19]

Unlike Paul, the pastoral writer only once names his opponents and enters into theological debate with them. Robert J. Karris has pointed out that there is a traditional schema behind the polemic of the Pastorals. The author borrows conventional criticisms from popular philosophy (his opponents are greedy, deceivers, quibblers, full of vice, unable to practice what they preach, quick to prey on women, and so forth) in an attempt to cause aversion toward his opponents and sympathy for his own point of view. This prevents us from having an accurate picture of the heretics; the author wants to prove that he alone has the right to, and actually does, impart truth.[20] "Thus we have in the Pastorals the paradoxical situation that false teachers are fiercely attacked, but we are left without any very clear picture of their doctrine; and the true teaching is to be carefully guarded, though we are never told precisely what it is."[21]

The link between the polemic against false teachers and the situation of the widows is provided by the church's increasing preoccupation with social acceptability. The author of the Pastorals is anxious that the church appear well to those outside it (1 Tim. 2:1-2; 5:14; 6:1-2; Titus 2:1-10). Apparently, Christianity's freedom from normal social patterns (as evidenced by Gal. 3:28) threatened *patria potestas* (*pater familias*), and therefore the whole Roman social order.

Thus the writer of the Pastorals wants to orient the church toward a patriarchal order of household duties (*haustafel*) similar to that of the dominant culture of the Roman Empire.

In *The Household of God,* David C. Verner convincingly argues that just as the household (*oikos*) was the basic unit of the church, the church was a social structure modeled on the household. He describes in detail the household in the Hellenistic-Roman world and concludes that "social tensions related to the household in this period appear to have centered around the changing position of women in society."[22] The traditional patriarchal household and the conventional sex roles "had come to be associated on a symbolic level with the preservation of an orderly and stable society. Consequently, people whose behavior defied the traditional values in this area risked the charge of political subversion."[23] Here Christianity enters with its message of freedom. As noted, the Pastorals evince a strong concern for the opinion of contemporary society. The church, in order to preserve its standing in the community, began to conform to the community's social norms. This is particularly evident in the admonitions to women in 1 Timothy 2 and 5[24] and in Titus 2. As the church clamped down on their freedom, women who had been attracted by that freedom moved into communities where they believed that original spirit to be preserved.

In a fresh look at 1 Tim. 5:3-16, Jouette Bassler depicts exactly this pattern. She notes that women turned to celibacy to find freedom from the inequalities imposed by marriage. Celibacy was required in the widows' circle, but women were thereby freed from patriarchal norms. "The widows of the Pastoral Epistles were, like the vestal virgins, under special restrictions, but again like the vestals, these restrictions were not those binding ordinary women. Indeed, widows were remarkably free of these ordinary restraints."[25] Bassler suggests that as the church became more willing to adapt to society's norms, the numbers in the widows' circle increased as women sought a degree of freedom.[26] The increasing number of widows was met by injunctions drawn from society's patriarchal norms. Criteria "were introduced for enrollment . . . that affirmed the very behavior from which the widows themselves were exempt—domesticity, marital fidelity, childbearing, etc."[27] The goal was to reduce the group by selecting only widows with the domestic virtues expected by contemporary society. The result, however, was an exacerbation of the heresy problem as women sought groups that presented equality, if not doctrinal purity.[28]

These problems faced by the church at the time of the writing of the Pastorals must be kept clearly in mind when one attempts to interpret any section of the letters. Church order, false teaching, and the tenuous position of the church in society after the severity of Domitian (d. A.D. 96) are all in the writer's mind as the material on widows in 1 Tim. 5:3-16 is presented. The sociological analyses of Verner, Bassler, and others provide an invaluable backdrop for the textual analysis to which we now turn.

1 TIMOTHY 5:3-16

Honor widows who are real widows. If a widow has children or grandchildren, let them first learn their religious duty to their own family and make some return to their parents; for this is acceptable in the sight of God. She who is a real widow, and is left all alone, has set her hope on God and continues in supplications and prayers night and day; whereas she who is self-indulgent is dead even while she lives. Command this, so that they may be without reproach. If any one does not provide for his relatives, and especially for his own family, he has disowned the faith and is worse than an unbeliever. Let a widow be enrolled if she is not less than sixty years of age, having been the wife of one husband; and she must be well attested for her good deeds, as one who has brought up children, shown hospitality, washed the feet of the saints, relieved the afflicted, and devoted herself to doing good in every way. But refuse to enrol younger widows; for when they grow wanton against Christ they desire to marry, and so they incur condemnation for having violated their first pledge. Besides that, they learn to be idlers, gadding about from house to house, and not only idlers but gossips and busybodies, saying what they should not. So I would have younger widows marry, bear children, rule their households, and give the enemy no occasion to revile us. For some have already strayed after Satan. If any believing woman has relatives who are widows, let her assist them; let the church not be burdened, so that it may assist those who are real widows.

Bassler has noted that many "of the difficulties presented by the text stem from the fact that the author is not initiating a new benevolence, which would have involved a more careful explanation of terms and conditions, but is seeking to limit an existing one."[29] This helpful suggestion is borne out by the evidence from Acts (see chap. 2, above), and it helps to explain the two general lines of interpretation of the passage.

The first, held by Joachim Jeremias, Gerhard Delling, and Hans-Werner Bartsch, argues that we are dealing with three sections: vv. 3-8 are on care of the widows; v. 9 begins a new section on requirements for office; and v. 16 is a distinct section. This view is supported by the lack of connectives between vv. 8-9 and vv. 15-16, by the fact that all needy widows must have been entitled to support, and by the fact that a younger widow who remarried would be excluding herself from becoming an official widow, but not from receiving the support of the church if the second husband died.[30]

The second, promulgated by Alexander Sand, J. Müller-Bardorff, and Dibelius/Conzelmann, argues that vv. 3-16 are a unified whole that addresses the problem of determining who is a "real" widow. The dual thrust of the imperative in v. 3 ("Honor") serves to restrict who the widows are and, therefore, vv. 4-16 are an explanation of real widows.[31]

Both readings imply that we are dealing with two groups, the enrolled widows (whether or not they form an "order") and those who were, by reason of family connection or age, ineligible to be enrolled (whether or not they received the support of the church). In the discussion that follows I assume (along with Jean Danielou, John Döllinger, W. H. C. Frend, Stählin, and Edward Schweizer[32]) that the widows are a special group with assigned duties or functions in the community. Along with Sand, I take the position that 1 Tim. 5:3-16 speaks of three groups of widows: "true" or enrolled widows, widows (usually older) who are not enrolled, and younger widows.[33] I think this threefold distinction clarifies the instructions regarding widows. This position stems not so much from textual considerations as from the instructions themselves. It rests upon the fact that the issue is not primarily one of age but of need.[34]

The first group, the true widows (tas ontōs charas), are discussed in 1 Tim. 5:3, 5-7, 9-10. They form the "order" and shall be dealt with in some detail presently. The second group are widows who are not enrolled because they have some other means of support. Verses 4, 8, and 16 discuss the case of these widows and suggest that, since they have children or grandchildren, they may be older (although this is not always the case). Bassler, Schüssler Fiorenza, and Verner have pointed out the financial problems that increasing numbers of widows created for the church.[35] The unenrolled widows, while they might be able and qualified to do the work of the order, are excluded on the basis of financial strain on the church. This, in fact, is the writer's leitmotif in the passage; it is the only injunction repeated three times, and it is repeated at evenly spaced intervals in the passage, which suggests to me the writer's premeditation. (In fact, if vv. 4, 8, and 16 are deleted, the material on the other two groups, the enrolled widows and the younger widows, falls into neat sections.)

Acts may provide an example of the unenrolled widow in the person of Tabitha, and Luke's Galilean women may afford another. There is also the example of Rigine, "mother, widow, who remained a widow sixty years and never burdened the Church; an *univira* who lived eighty years, five months, twenty-six days." Significantly, her daughter "nicely made this stone."[36] Presumably about twenty years old when she became a widow, Rigine supported her family and then was supported by her children, or at least by her daughter, who was wealthy enough to erect a monument for her.

The third group of widows in the passage are the young widows of 5:11-15. They bring into focus the problems of the attitude of the larger society toward the church ("Give the enemy no occasion to revile us," v. 14) and of false teachers ("They learn to be . . . not only idlers but gossips and busybodies, saying what they should not," v. 13; "Some have already strayed after Satan," v. 16). In his commentary on the pastoral epistles, E. F. Scott notes that no charges against the church were more effective than those regarding the character of its women.[37] Antiquity generally had high admiration for young, chaste widows.[38] Not only here, but also in Titus 2:4-5 (where older women are to teach the younger women), the writer of the Pastorals stresses the traditional, domestic virtues that would be acceptable and praiseworthy in order that "the word of God may not be discredited" (2:5b). "Younger women are to follow the societal and legal requirements for women of their age so that the Christian reputation will be preserved."[39] Remarriage is encouraged in spite of Paul's advice in 1 Corinthians 7 that "she is happier if she remains as she is."

As we noted earlier, the problem of the church's status in the community was tied to its internal problems with false teaching. In dealing with the younger widows, the writer's interest "is not merely a civil apologetic interest."[40] Barrett notes that the service the widows rendered (pastoral house calls) presented temptations the young could not withstand.[41] The most serious of these for the church was contact with and spreading of false teaching. "Paul" begins by telling Timothy that he may "charge certain persons not to teach any different doctrine, nor to occupy themselves with myths and endless genealogies which promote speculations rather than the divine training that is in faith" (1 Tim. 1:3-4). Schüssler Fiorenza provides the link to the young widows:

> The author does not say what it was that the widows were saying during these home visits. . . . The opponents' teaching is based on "deceitful preaching by liars" who "forbid marriage and demand abstinence from food" (1 Tim. 4:2-4). Timothy is admonished to "reject the profane stories told by old women" (4:7). That the opponents had especially good relationships and success with women is stressed in 2 Tim. 3:6-9: they make their way into households and persuade "idle" or "little" women, who are negatively labeled as "overwhelmed with sins and driven by all kinds of desires."[42]

The exact nature of the opponents' teaching has not been agreed upon, but it is usually assumed that the opponents were men. It is certainly possible that there were also women among them, perhaps from the group of young widows. "Apparently the author cannot prove that [they] taught anything heretical, but that their whole lifestyle corresponded to that taught by the opponent teachers."[43]

The false teachers were having a success that the pastoral writer discredits by calling into question the good sense of the women. Prohibition against marriage was apparently a prominent feature of the false teachers (see 1 Tim. 4:3). Such teaching calls to mind the sexual asceticism of the Apocryphal Acts, especially the *Acts of Paul* which, in the person of Thecla, contains tendencies toward female emancipation.[44] Dennis MacDonald argues that the Pastorals were, in fact, written to refute oral stories that Paul had commissioned women to teach. Thus, to limit the number of widows would be to limit the number of tale-bearers who carried a message that would upset the "household order."[45]

In conclusion, then, the young widows were problematic to the church leadership because they were drawn to "false teaching" that

offered them emancipation in the household and leadership opportunities in the church. Verner nicely sums up the situation:

> Younger widows emerge . . . as rather dangerous and unpredictable
> beings who should be controlled in marriage, rather than given official
> status in the church. The description thus suggests that these women
> were the focus of real social tensions involving a conflict of values over
> the role of women in the household and the community.[46]

THE ORDER

Having examined some of the issues connected with unenrolled
widows and younger widows, we now turn to the "enrolled widows"
who made up the "order." Stählin notes that in 1 Tim. 5:3-15 we
find what "might be called the earliest Christian order for widows.
Its climax is the institution of congregational widows, *ontōs chērai,*
from whom two other groups of widows . . . are distinguished."[47]
The material on the "real widows" is drawn primarily, though not
exclusively, from vv. 3, 5-7, 9-10.

It is now appropriate to raise the question of textual evidence for
an "order." The key arguments include the context in 1 Timothy, the
terms *tima,* "honor" (v. 3), and *katalegesthō,* "let . . . be enrolled" (v.
9), and the suggestion of a *pistin* (vow or pledge, v. 12). Hanson has
suggested that the Pastorals are addressed to church leaders and not
to the church at large.[48] This may account for the roster of church
officials in 1 Timothy. The writer lists qualifications for bishops in
3:1-7, deacons in 3:8-13,[49] elders in 5:17-19, and, by implication,
teachers (throughout the letters). The widows appear in the midst of
the roster of officials (5:3-16). "This parallelism, then, suggests that
enrolled widows too are church officials."[50] The special nature of the
group is indicated by its separate listing. Their service "is so important
to the Church that we hear almost as much about it as about that of
the bishops."[51]

Although the phrase "real widows" itself suggests the delineation
of a special category, the scholarly debate about 1 Tim. 5:3, and
especially the term *tima,* is lively. The general meaning of *tima* is
"honor," "respect," or "value," but it can also mean "pay" or "com-
pensation." In the later church orders, *timan* is a technical term for
payment.[52] Several scholars (e.g., Dibelius and Conzelmann, Josef
Ernst, Sand, Verner)[53] maintain that at the writing of the Pastorals

the term does not yet suggest support by the congregation. Others (Barrett, Stählin) assume the more technical meaning here.[54]

Sirach (written about 180 B.C. and translated into Greek about 132 B.C.) uses the term *tima* in the sense of "pay": "Honor [*tima*] the physician with the honor [*timais*] due him" (38:1). Scholars who insist on Pauline authorship of the Pastorals note its Jewish elements. While I do not hold this thesis, the Jewish tradition is clear. Several fragments of the Hebrew text of Sirach dating from around the time of Jesus have been found in the Qumran documents. The work is certainly characteristic of the Judaism that became the rabbinical schools. The point for our discussion is that the term *tima* was used in a technical sense in the religious literature studied at the time of the Pastorals. (Certainly Sirach would have been included in the "sacred writings" mentioned in 2 Tim. 3:15.) This fact leads me to accept readings that favor the more technical rendering of *tima* in 1 Tim. 5:3.

Much has been made of the use of the term *katalegein*, "to enroll," in 1 Tim. 5:9. Dibelius and Conzelmann point out that in parallel literature *katalegein* is a technical term for the registration of levied troops.[55] Stählin says the term means "to be adopted into a fellowship by election," and notes that the requirements for selection immediately follow.[56] Walter Lock suggests the widows were "placed on a list of those who were pledged . . . to life-long widowhood."[57] These suggestions lead me to conclude, with Bartsch, that in 5:9-16 we have the foundation of the widows' regulations.[58]

Although 1 Tim. 5:12, 14 is, strictly speaking, in the section on younger widows, the language there also suggests an office. Verner believes "first trust" or "first faith," *tēn protēn pistin*, refers to "an initial oath of celibacy taken by widows on the occasion of their enrollment."[59] Both Barrett and Easton agree that a woman enrolled as a widow took a special pledge. Barrett describes it as an "undertaking . . . not to marry, but to engage herself wholly to the Church."[60] Easton goes further and asserts that the widows pledged themselves to Christ so that a subsequent marriage would be infidelity to him.[61] If the latter reading is correct, then the passage not only initiates the order of widows but is the biblical root of modern religious orders for women. Finally, *boulomai*, "I would have" or "it is my wish," is

more than a resolute formulation; the term is used regularly in leg-
islative regulations and official decrees.[62]

None of these textual elements by itself proves the establishment
of an order of widows in 1 Tim. 5:3-16. Taken together, however,
they make a good case. Furthermore, the text clearly enumerates four
requirements (and suggests a fifth) for joining the order, and it points
clearly to tasks its members are to undertake on behalf of the church.

Döllinger's summary on the widows in 1 Timothy provides a useful
overview of the qualifications of a "real widow." These women, he
notes, "had a special relation to the church. Their names were to be
marked in a catalogue, and they were to have a special ministry
assigned to them."[63] Requisite conditions for enrollment included that
the woman be over sixty years of age and the wife of one husband,
and that she have witnesses to her good works, skill with children,
hospitality, and compassion. In short, the widow was to be chaste
and devout and to have female accomplishments acceptable to the
larger community.

The text sets out the first complex of qualifications for widows in
vv. 5-7. She must be alone (and thus dependent upon God and not
persons); and she must be continually faithful ("continues in supplications," v. 5) and chaste (not "self-indulgent," v. 6). We have
discussed the question of other means of support previously. "First
Timothy repeats three times that widows who have relatives must be
assisted by them so that the Church . . . may use her resources to
support the 'real widows.' "[64]

That the widow's hope is in God is a direct inheritance from the
Old Testament. As we noted in chapter 1, the God of Israel has special
concern for the powerless (strangers, widows, orphans). To cite but
one example, in Jer. 49:11b the Lord of hosts declares, "Let your
widows trust in me." The widows' supplications are especially effective because God is listening for them.

The faithfulness and chastity mentioned in vv. 5-6 reflect the preoccupation of the non-Christian world with continence. In Cynic-Stoic
diatribes continence is crucial to the ideal of the detached "wise man."
Asceticism reached its highest point in Neoplatonism; the first step
to perfection was to subdue the body. Evidence for the lofty regard
for virginity in the early church (Matt. 19:29; 1 Cor. 7:7-9, 32-34)
stands in contrast to the Jewish tradition, which viewed fecundity as

a special mark of God's favor.[65] The command that the widows be chaste and continent, then, demonstrates the church's concern about society's opinion of it. Verse 6 may well allude to a proverb or adage in general use at the time,[66] or it may reflect a fear in the Hellenistic world that widowhood would lead to prostitution.[67] But the command in v. 7 emphasizes that the church's conduct must be above reproach. Commenting on this text, Barrett writes, "All members of the church should be free of reproach, but it is particularly important that this should be true of those who hold public position within it, and draw their support from it."[68]

"Let a widow be enrolled" (v. 9) implies that qualifications will follow. Three qualifications do: age; marital status; and the general category of "good deeds," followed by specific examples of these deeds.

A modern reader of 1 Timothy might ask why sixty years of age is set as the lower limit for enrollment. Several possibilities suggest themselves. First, sixty was the average age of the "elderly" in ancient literature. Generally speaking, people did not live as long then as they do now, so sixty was a relatively advanced age. Furthermore, since it was the practice for men to marry women who were much younger, there were younger widows (vv. 11-15) who required guidance, and these were to be excluded from the order.[69] Practically speaking, a woman of sixty would have mature experience of life and be subject to less sexual peril in performing her duties. As we shall see, the duties spelled out here for widows could be discharged without undue exertion. Perhaps, too, the writer assumes a woman of sixty to be less mobile than her younger sisters and, thus, beyond the dangers to the church connected with "gadding about from house to house" (v. 13). However, since there is evidence that some of the widows carried on charitable and pastoral visitation on the church's behalf, and that wealthy widows took charge of house churches, we are wise not to push this conclusion too far.

The requirement that the widow have been the wife of one husband is tied to the social norms of the time. A frequent theme in sagas and stories in ancient literature is the flighty widow who moves from her dead husband to a new relationship (see, for example, the matron of Ephesus in Petronius's *Satyricon*).[70] Such a woman was an object of scorn. In our treatment of widows in the Roman world (see chap. 1

above) it was noted that *univira* became an epithet for a good wife
and that from being used to praise a woman who married once it
and *monandros* came to praise chastity for the love of God.

The parallel phrases "the husband of one wife" and "the wife of
one husband" appear several times in the pastoral epistles (1 Tim.
3:2, 12; 5:9; Titus 1:6), always as a qualification for office (bishop,
deacon, widow, and elder, respectively). Scholars offer several explanations of the phrases, but the most reasonable explanations concern the church's growing tendency to frown on second marriages
(even though the author encourages them in 5:14!) and the possibility
that the prohibition is directed at a church official who has divorced
a previous spouse and remarried.[71] The apparent discrepancy between
these two explanations is lessened when one recognizes that each
sees the church as seeking practical ways to preserve its moral standing in the eyes of the larger community.

After continence, age, and marital status, evidence of a life of active
service is the fourth qualification of "real widows." Verse 10 opens
and closes with the phrase "doing good." It is interesting to note that
two of three examples of "good works" (hospitality and raising children) are domestic activities from which the widow in an order, by
virtue of her single life, may be excluded. Each is considered an
acceptable female activity in Greco-Roman society.

In this context, the work of Karen Torjesen is enlightening. She
has carefully studied treatises on Greco-Roman household management. In these treatises, the role of the husband is to bring in wealth
from outside and the role of the wife is to manage goods and persons
inside the house (*oikos*). We have already noted how the church
adopted household codes as its organization developed. Torjesen suggests that leadership roles in the church were based on leadership
roles in the house. Thus, as long as the church was "private" (i.e.,
in the house), there were no barriers to women in roles of leadership.
Exclusion of women from leadership occurred when the church
moved from the house (*oikos*) to the city-state (*polis*).[72] The "good
deeds" in 1 Tim. 5:10 all concern household management. To apply
Torjesen's theory, then, each would help to qualify a woman for
leadership in the church. Recall that the Pastorals are late-first-century
or early-second-century documents. Until the middle of the third
century, the worship of the church was in private homes. Thus 1

Timothy is part of the literature of the house church, not the post-Constantinian city-state church.

In connection with specific "good deeds," Scott has suggested that "as one who has brought up children" need not refer to a woman's own children,[73] and Müller-Bardorff understands the same phrase to mean that teaching children was one of the widow's tasks.[74] The spiritual quality embodied in the phrase is nurturance. "Hospitality" embodies generosity and openness; and foot washing embodies humility. A person moved to relieve the distress of those in trouble is compassionate. In short, 1 Tim. 5:10 is discussing spiritual attributes and not specific acts that the writer, as a Christian, requires of a widow (although the specific acts would be acceptable to society). These attitudes, and not each and every "work," are the prerequisites for "real widows." "Women were needed who would perform the lowliest duties on behalf of others, in the spirit which Christ Himself had taught by His example."[75]

Behind the "good deeds" required of widows stand the words of Jesus: "If I then, your Lord and Teacher, have washed your feet, you also ought to wash one another's feet" (John 13:14). The "real widows" will be expected to follow the example of humble service set by Christ. They will be to the church what the woman with the ointment was to Jesus in Luke 7:36-50. As we argue that women held positions of leadership in the early church, we do well to remember that from the beginning of the church the primary characteristics of all Christian leaders have been humility and willingness to serve. In the kingdom, "service is not a stepping stone to nobility; it is . . . the only kind of nobility that is recognized."[76]

In addition to the four qualifications taken from the passages on "real widows" (continence, vv. 5-7; age and marital status, v. 9; and attested good works, v. 10), there is in v. 12 (on younger widows) the implication that a vow or pledge (*pistin*) is expected of "real widows." Their willingness to take it is both the final qualification for the order and the means of enrollment in it. Many scholars think that the Greek verb *katalegein,* "to enroll" (v. 9), is a technical term for the enrollment process. Thus, "first pledge" (v. 12) refers to a vow taken upon enrollment, a vow of celibacy or of fidelity to Christ in service to his church. "Thus having violated their first pledge does not refer merely to the fact that they have taken . . . a second husband, but that they have broken the vow which they took on joining the order, whereby they became devoted to Christ instead of a husband."[77] This vow must have been intended to secure in practice the chaste life described in vv. 5-6.

If, as I have suggested, the pastoral writer lists qualifications for an office, then it is logical to suppose that those enrolled in this office will have special responsibilities or duties. Schweizer concurs and notes that the "widow is supposed to have performed diaconal services before she is received as widow. That may lead one to suppose that she continues to perform such services; but that is by no means certain, and it is not demanded explicitly here."[78] While the duties of the widow are not explicitly listed (in 1 Tim. 5:3-16 the writer intends to enumerate the tests of life before enrollment, not to initiate an order or to list its duties), several are clearly implied. The fact that no duties are spelled out does not mean there was no office. As Verner notes, no duties were spelled out for deacons,[79] and the existence of that office is not questioned.

The first duty of the widows is undoubtedly prayer and intercession (v. 5). To "pray continually" is, of course, enjoined of all Christians, but the widows of the church have before them the special example of Anna (Luke 2:36-38). Furthermore, Jean La Porte observes that the early church especially encouraged the elderly to engage in a life of contemplation. "The key to understanding the ideals offered to the elderly by the Early Church lies in the association of continence, fasting, and prayer—or the renunciation of the flesh for the sake of the spiritual life."[80] "All the Elderly . . . were invited to renounce activity and to spend more time on meditation and prayer."[81]

Several New Testament passages associate continence, fasting, and prayer in the Christian life (see, for example, Acts 13:2-3; 1 Cor. 7:5). Why should these qualities be especially appropriate for the elderly? First, physical deterioration, a normal part of the aging process, precludes more active service. Anyone, regardless of physical condition, can pray. Second, those who believe a primary qualification for the order is need might argue that destitution makes widows more likely to devote themselves to prayer, since they have no means for acts of benevolence. (And, presumably, the hunger of the elderly poor is thereby transformed into religious fasting!) Third, from a practical standpoint, freedom from the domestic duties connected with maintaining a family gives the widows more time for public and private devotion. Scholarly evidence suggests that widows made up a majority of the weekday community of worship, just as they do now. (Referring to the situation in the middle of the third century, Eusebius notes that "more than 1500 widows and persons in distress" were supported by the church in Rome.)[82]

The strongest reason for assigning the duty of intercession to the widows is not practical but theological. Jesus concludes the parable of the unjust judge by saying, "And will not God vindicate his elect, who cry to him day and night?" (Luke 18:7). Faith (hope in God) is a prerequisite to persistent prayer. The widow has no one else on whom to depend. According to Sirach, God's ears are especially attuned to hear persons totally dependent upon God; God's preference is for the poor and destitute:

> He will not ignore the supplication of the fatherless,
>   nor the widow when she pours out her story . . .
> The prayer of the humble pierces the clouds, and he will not
>   be consoled until it reaches the Lord.
>
>   (Sir. 35:14, 17)

The church's prayers are at the top of the list of widow's tasks because, since she is totally dependent upon God, God will be most likely to hear prayers from her lips.

The second duty of the "real widows" is suggested by the fact that the younger widows are scolded for "gadding about from house to house" (v. 13). Dibelius and Conzelmann assume this going about was in the context of house calls.[83] The nature of the visits the widows were expected to make as part of their duties is not indicated, but it must have been charitable and pastoral. Perhaps it was connected with the teaching function mentioned in Titus 2:3-5.

In 1 Tim. 5:13, the phrase "they learn to be idlers" has troubled scholars. Some scholars argue that this, together with "busybodies," is a reference to Acts 19:19 and the burning of books of magic. In the course of visitation some of the women were uttering spells and incantations ("speaking what they should not").[84] I find this an ingenious but unconvincing exegesis. In terms of literary archetype, certainly the old women would be more likely to be accused of necromancy. However, 1 Tim. 5:13 implies that widows are the ones

responsible for visitation. Perhaps they were teaching women who
were confined to their homes by domestic responsibility.

Teaching does not appear in 1 Tim. 5:3-16 (unless we extract it
from "bringing up children" in v. 10); we are not, however, without
other textual evidence for considering that possibility here. Titus 2
deals with the promulgation of sound doctrine (orthodox catechesis)
in the church. It addresses the older men, the older women, the young
women, the young men, and slaves. Schweizer notes that in the
"sociological group of the older church members . . . those who perform a special ministry are referred to more and more clearly as *the*
'older men,' just as among the widows *the* 'widows' appear as a special
group."[85] We can read "older women," *presbytidas,* in Titus 2:3 in
this light.

First, there is almost exact correspondence between the qualities
required of an "older woman" here, and those required of a woman
deacon in 1 Tim. 3:11. The equation of the offices of deaconess and
widow occurred very early; it is an issue we shall address later. What
sometimes appears to be interchangeable use of the terms "deaconess" and "widow" has made it difficult to trace exactly the development of either office.[86] Second, there is inscriptional evidence for
a technical use of *presbytis.* "An epitaph for Kale *pre(s)b(ytis)* is re-
printed . . . (Centuripae, Sicily; IV/V). Another with this title is probably referred to in one of the so-called Angels of Thera inscriptions:
Aggelos Epiktous presbytidos (III-V)."[87] G. W. H. Lampe uses this text
as evidence of an office-bearer ("senior widow"), as well as for the
adjectival sense "elderly woman." It seems logical to conclude that
these older female officeholders might well be the widows whom the
pastoral writer addresses earlier (as K. H. Schaefer also suggests).[88]

These older women are to serve the church as teachers of the
younger women, teachers of good (*kalodisdaskalous*). Not surprisingly,
the good to be taught involves, according to Titus 2:4-5, acceptable
female behavior: sensibility, chastity, domesticity, kindness, submis-
siveness to husbands, "that the word of God may not be discredited"
(v. 5). (The young women are to be taught the same responsibilities
as slaves, to keep a proper place at home and not give Christianity
a bad name in public.)[89] If this is the substance of the widow's message, it is even more crucial for her to have lived the life described
in 1 Tim. 5:10.

That the pastoral writer is limiting an existing order rather than instituting a new one explains the scant information on the duties of the order; it is assumed that readers know them. Since we do not know the duties, we can only speculate by drawing out the implications of relevant texts. Thus, 1 Tim. 5:3-16 suggests that the "real widows" were primarily to lead a contemplative life of prayer, but might also be called upon to make pastoral house calls. Titus 2:3-5 introduces the possibility that the widows taught proper Christian conduct and attitudes to younger women.

One final possibility should be mentioned. Stählin believes wealthy widows took charge of house churches.[90] We have mentioned Tabitha and her responsibility for less fortunate widows (see chap. 2). If we use the general definition of *chēra* ("a woman living without a husband") and make the standard assumption that women mentioned alone had no husbands, then there are several widows with house churches, among them Mary, the mother of John Mark (Acts 12:12), and Lydia (Acts 16:11-15). Archaeological evidence from the Jewish community suggests that the religious leadership of women was sometimes connected with their financial support of the community. Theopempta of Myndos is called *archisynagogos* (leader of synagogue). As the inscription uses no family surnames ("son of," "wife of," etc.), it is assumed she had no husband. The Roman tombstone of Vetruia Paucla says she was *mater* (mother) of two synagogues.[91] Since we have the examples of Tabitha and Lydia, there is no reason to doubt similar patronage by Christian widows (even those of pagan background) of the church. According to our schema, however, these may not have been enrolled widows; patronage cannot have been a requirement for an order if need was one of the prerequisites for enrollment.

CONCLUSIONS

Any reading of 1 Tim. 5:3-16 must take into account the situation of the church at the beginning of the second century, particularly the problems connected with church order, false teaching, and social pressure. The widows are listed in a roster of church officials. Of those officials (bishop, deacon, deaconess, widow, elder) only the widows are limited with regard to support, finances, and sexual continence. This reinforces the theory promulgated by Bassler and others that the writer is limiting an already existing "institution." (Evidence from Acts suggests that the widows were, indeed, in evidence at an earlier stage in the church's development.)

Exegesis of the passage is complicated by the fact that the passage seems to treat at least three groups of widows: "real widows" (those dependent upon and enrolled in the order); widows with another means of support; and young widows (who are encouraged to re-marry, would not be excluded from support if it were needed, but could not be enrolled). In addition to the context in 1 Timothy, several terms and phrases give textual evidence for an order.

The requirements of that order included that a woman have no other means of support (though this point is debated), be at least sixty years of age, have been the wife of one husband, and have attested good deeds of domesticity, hospitality, humility, and com-passion. It is possible, though not certain, that she was expected to take a vow of enrollment by which she pledged fidelity to Christ and his church. These requirements were strict enough to limit the number of enrolled widows and thus relieve the financial burden on the church, prevent the embarrassment caused to the church when younger widows broke the pledge of celibacy, and limit the number of older women "telling tales" (RSV, "gossips") or spreading false doctrine.[92]

While seeking to limit the number of widows the church had to support, the pastoral writer still gave assent to the practice of helping needy widows and continued their office.[93] In return for support, the widows were to lead a life of contemplation and of intercession for the church. It is possible that some of the widows made charitable and pastoral house calls and taught younger women "what is good." As with so much about the order at this time, however, the duties, especially those of calling and teaching, are speculation on our part.

Nevertheless, it is clear from the pastoral letters that an office for older women not only existed in the church but was large and active enough to require detailed regulation. "The term 'widow' becomes so generic for the office that Ignatius (*Smyrnaeans* 13.1) can speak unconcernedly of 'the virgins who are called *widows*,' obviously meaning the unmarried women who are doing the same work as the 'widows.' "[94] Easton's remark both indicates that the widows will be prominent in the writings of the Apostolic Fathers and foreshadows a problem that has plagued scholars, namely, the imprecision with which the term "widow" is used. As we turn to the Apostolic Fathers, we shall have to be on the lookout for virgins, widows, *and* deacons!

4

The Apostolic Period

INTRODUCTION

The pastoral epistles rightly belong to the literature of the second-century church. Their concern for establishing offices of ministry and for preventing heretical contamination of the church's doctrine prefigures the major issues of that century. No other century is so crucial in the church's development. The second-century church saw the rise of the monepiscopacy and the beginnings of a movement toward a canon of Scripture; it faced challenges from Gnosticism, Marcionism, and Montanism that shaped modern orthodoxy. Danielou, Frend, B. H. Streeter, and others have pointed out that the church developed around large urban centers, with an almost bewildering array of variations of "orthodox" Christianity.[1] Streeter correctly asserts that the "history of Catholic Christianity during the first five centuries is the history of a progressive standardization of a diversity which had its origin in the Apostolic age."[2]

Nor was the church exempt from the slings and arrows of political life in its development. Still reeling from its treatment by the Roman emperor Domitian (81–96) and his interest in promoting his own cult (an ambition so strong that it led him to persecute members of his own family), the church was faced with Trajan (98–117). While Trajan was a praiseworthy emperor, he was ignorant of the nature of Christianity and included it in general legislation against secret societies. This decision regulated governmental treatment of Christians for most of the second century.[3] We gain much information about early Christianity in Asia Minor from Trajan's correspondence with Pliny, governor of Bithynia from 109 to 111, but Trajan's rule also resulted in the martyrdom of Ignatius of Antioch. The strength of Christianity in Egypt, Syria, Rome, and provincial Asia led to relatively peaceful official relations with the empire under Hadrian (117–38) and Antionius Pious (137–61). There was, however, no change in the legal status of Christianity, and popular opinion toward it in the Greek-speaking world was becoming hostile.

Under Marcus Aurelius (161–80) this hostility ignited and Christians became public enemies of the city-state. Frend calls the period from 160 to 185 a "generation of crisis."[4] Perhaps because Marcus Aurelius was a philosopher-king (an eminently reasonable Stoic) he had no sympathy for Christianity. Under his rule the church lost Polycarp of Smyrna, Justin of Rome, and an untold number in Gaul to martyrdom. Marcus Aurelius's son Commodus (180–92) was completely depraved but tolerated Christians (because, it has been suggested, of a concubine, Marcia).[5] At the close of the century, Septimus Severus (193–211) enacted laws against the spread of both Judaism and Christianity, so the century ended as it had begun, with a "flowering" of martyrdoms.

When we turn to the Fathers whom Cecil J. Cadoux calls the "earlier apologists,"[6] we must bear in mind the adverse political climate. It helps to account for the new emphasis in the church on celibacy, virginity, and sexual abstinence, as well as for prohibitions against second marriages. Persons in danger of being dragged away to the lions will need greater consolations than those provided by normal human relations!

We have mentioned heterodox sects and the canon only in passing. Both relate to our discussion of widows because of the role women played in such sects. Evidence of the importance of women in the gnostic, Nicolaitan, Naasene, and especially Montanist sects is found in many of the Apocryphal Acts and so-called gospels. In a study of the Apocryphal Acts, *The Revolt of the Widows,* S. L. Davies notes,

> Scholars often dismiss the Acts from serious consideration as evidence about Christians of the first centuries of the church. In doing so they dismiss a substantial percentage of all early Christian documents. . . . The apocryphal Acts are testimonies to varieties of Christian belief and to a particular way of life. They derive from common people who agreed on the proper way of living for Christians but had differing doctrinal opinions.[7]

Fortunately for church history (especially that dealing with the role of women), recent scholarship has begun to look again at material once considered at best dangerous and at worst useless. Davies's own work examines in detail the relationship between the widows and the Apocryphal Acts and concludes that the latter derive from communities of continent women. He notes that the Apocryphal Acts come from the transitional period, when charismatic leadership in the church was moving toward the institutional and opportunities for women to obtain leadership roles in the church were diminishing. These Acts, which he believes were written by women in communities, take the form they do because of the limited way women were allowed to express themselves in the larger church.[8] Davies, in fact, thinks the Apocryphal Acts constitute a body of literature produced by the order of widows, and his conclusion is to some degree corroborated by MacDonald's essay "Virgins, Widows, and Paul in Second Century Asia Minor."[9]

Although Ross Kraemer's work is not concerned with authorship of the Apocryphal Acts, it also demonstrates the appeal of ascetic and heterodox Christianity to women, particularly in the eastern provinces of the Roman Empire. As Bassler concluded about the widows in 1 Timothy, Kraemer concludes that women who found traditional roles inadequate looked to ascetic Christianity for higher standards of worth.[10] Elaine Pagels thinks gnostic Christians built an equality principle into the social and political structure of their communities in striking opposition to the orthodox pattern; by the late second century orthodox communities assumed the domination of men over women not only for social and family life but also for the church.[11] Of the apocryphal materials, much work has been done on the *Acts of Paul and Thecla* (to which Tertullian referred about A.D. 200) because of the character of Thecla and the possibility that she accompanied Paul, taught, and baptized.[12]

The reason for this brief digression on the apocryphal writings and heretical sects of the second century is to point out that, although we are not treating them here, there is ample material available to fill in the gaps which are admittedly left when we choose to deal only with what the church has come to call "orthodox" sources. (Studies by Davies, Roger Gryson, MacDonald, Pagels, Schüssler Fiorenza, and others preclude the need to cover this ground again, and the reader is encouraged to consult these studies for more information.)

Turning then to the Apostolic Fathers, by reviewing references made to the widows by Clement, Ignatius, Polycarp, and the Shepherd of Hermas we shall gain a sense of the prevailing opinion about the order in the early second century. We shall also come to know something of the order's condition in Asia and Syria, thus placing ourselves in the mainstream of church history, which insists that the cultural surroundings determined in large measure the development of the various forms of Christianity. Although Clement of Rome and the Shepherd of Hermas mention the widows only in passing, they give evidence of the widows in Rome.

CLEMENT OF ROME

The writings of Clement of Rome shed little light on the position of widows. According to Eusebius, Clement was bishop of Rome from the twelfth year of Domitian's reign (c. A.D. 92) to the third year of Trajan's (c. 101). Tertullian tells us that Clement was consecrated by Peter; Irenaeus tells us that Clement was Peter's third successor as bishop of Rome. While very little that is certain is known about Clement, the first letter to Corinth (*1 Clement*), which tradition attributes to him, is the earliest document outside the canon which can be dated. General agreement among scholars suggests it belongs to the last decade of the first century.

First Clement itself was probably occasioned by schism in the Corinthian church. It was not unusual for the leaders of one church to send advice to those of another. Paul set a precedent followed by Ignatius, Polycarp, Dionysius of Corinth, and others.[13] The letter from Rome to Corinth makes no claim to superior authority but does show Rome as a peacemaker among churches. It objects to the dismissal of certain presbyters, sets forth an argument for apostolic succession, and ends with a long eucharistic prayer. "The most striking feature of Clement's letter is its blending of Old Testament and Christian themes with Hellenistic ideas and expressions."[14] It makes numerous references to the Septuagint for illustration and sees in the heroes of Israel patterns for Christian conduct.

Clement's reference to the widows (*1 Clement* VIII. 4) occurs in such a context. Clement recalls Ezekiel's and Isaiah's calls for repentance and quotes the instructions in Isa. 1:16-20:

> Wash you, and make you clean, put away your wickedness from your souls before my eyes, cease from your wickedness, learn to do good, seek out judgment, rescue the wronged, give judgment for the orphan, do justice to the widow and come and let us reason together. (*1 Clement* VIII.4; cf. Isa. 1:16-20)[15]

The quotation exemplifies Clement's method and places his use of the prophetic material about widows squarely in the biblical tradition described earlier, but it does little to illuminate our knowledge of the widows except to remind us that they still needed the community's protection to receive just treatment.

IGNATIUS OF ANTIOCH

In the letters of Ignatius of Antioch we begin to get a sense of the extent to which the early church gave attention to her widows. The letters were written during the reign of Trajan, when Ignatius, having been sentenced to death, was marched from Antioch to Rome. Except for Ignatius's *Letter to the Romans,* his general purpose was to thank the various churches for the kindnesses extended to him.

Three concerns dominate the letters: Ignatius's approaching martyrdom, the unity of the church (manifested in part by instructions to its leaders), and heretical movements that inevitably lead to schism. Ignatius is the first writer outside the New Testament to describe Christ in philosophic categories current in his day, and is the first writer to stress the virgin birth.

Because it bears directly upon our study of the widows, a brief digression on the offices of ministry in the church of the early second century is in order here. Note first that we cannot fully reconcile differing accounts of the ministry in Clement, Ignatius, and the *Didache.* Most scholars attribute the differences to the development of the church in Jerusalem versus that in the Diaspora, noting that the organization in the Diaspora was looser.[16] The terms "bishop," "priest," and "deacon" (as well as the "functions" of apostle, prophet, and teacher) are not used uniformly to refer to the same responsibilities in the community. For example, "bishop" may mean "overseer," its literal meaning in synagogue parlance, or it may mean "priest" as it was used of Eleazar in Num. 4:16.[17] The term is used at least fifty-five times in the genuine letters of Ignatius. His letters show that bishops, supported by a council of presbyters and assisted by deacons, were in authority in the towns he visited in Asia Minor.

Here is a stage of development beyond that of the Pastorals; the single bishop is the leading figure in the church, apparently representing the "localizing of the teaching, ruling, and prophetic functions of the original missionary ministry of apostles, prophets, and catechists."[18] The office is the earthly antitype of a heavenly pattern: the bishop represents God; the presbyters, the apostles; the deacons, Christ; and so on. Such analogies will become important to us when the widow is included in the clerical list.

Thus, when offices of ministry are mentioned in the Apostolic Fathers, we must be careful to discern the meaning of the office mentioned in the particular community being addressed. For Ignatius, the interest is not so much in the form of ministry as in the unity of the church; he focuses on the ministry as a way to secure it.

Ignatius's references to the widows occur in his last three letters, *Letter to the Philadelphians, Letter to the Smyrnaeans,* and *Letter to Polycarp.* Apparently written from Troas, the letters are addressed to churches Ignatius actually visited and discuss the issues of unity and heresy, reflecting the problems of false teaching in detail. Of the seven Ignatian epistles attested by Eusebius, we have two Greek versions of each, a longer and a shorter. Scholars have generally accepted the shorter forms as genuine, although the debate on this point continues.[19] The textual issue is important for our study because the reference to widows in *Letter to the Philadelphians* occurs only in the longer version. Even if the longer version is the work of a later editor, it provides important information about the thinking of church officials in regard to widows in Asia Minor.

Letter to the Philadelphians interests us because it indicates the nature of "Judaistic" errors and gives snippets of a debate Ignatius carried on with the Judaizers (8.2). Chapter 4 of the longer edition gives instruction about the widows. The shorter version is a teaching on the unity of the Eucharist and enjoins the use of one cup to show the unity of Christians. This unity is also reflected in one altar and one bishop.

The longer version uses the closing exhortation of the shorter—

"that whatever you do you may do it according to God"—as an occasion to launch into an extended discussion of relationships within the household of faith. Wives, virgins, children, husbands, and fathers are given instructions (largely paraphrases of Pauline epistles) about how to conduct themselves in relation to one another. The section closes with a chain of obedience: governors to Caesar, soldiers to their superiors, deacons to presbyters, and all these to the bishop, who is obedient to Christ; "thus unity is preserved throughout." Immediately after the ranking of clergy comes the instruction for widows:

> Let not the widows be wanderers about, nor fond of dainties, nor gadders from house to house; but let them be like Judith, noted for her seriousness; and like Anna eminent for her sobriety.[20]

The writer places the widows after the list of clergy and not in the context of domestic relationships. "Virgins," which later denotes an order like (or perhaps overlapping with) the widows, here appears in connection with instructions to married persons. This suggests that their primary role was defined in terms of sexual continence and not yet in terms of service rendered or function performed in the Christian community.

Several concerns expressed by the writer echo those of the pastoral epistles. "Gadders from house to house" clearly echoes 1 Tim. 5:13, and the concern with wandering about may be connected to the idea of idleness expressed in 1 Timothy or with seeking money as in the *Didascalia* (XV), where widows are criticized for going from house to house in search of money. Being enjoined not to be fond of dainties suggests there must have been widows who exhibited a taste that was rather too delicate and refined for persons dependent upon the gifts of the community. Perhaps some widows were overly fastidious or even squeamish about their allotments. It is hard to imagine how the widows would be self-indulgent with respect to material things; the advice must be in connection with the widows' reception of gifts for their maintenance.

Judith and Anna are held up as models of behavior for the widows. We have discussed Anna at length earlier (see chap. 2). Judith is the pious widow in the Apocrypha who entices and then assassinates the Assyrian, Holofernes. After her husband's death by sunstroke, Judith "lived at home as a widow for three years and four months" fasting, and "no one spoke ill of her, for she feared God with great devotion" (Jth. 8:4, 8). She instructs the elders of her city, who admit it is not the first time her wisdom has been apparent because her "heart's disposition is right" (8:29). After Judith delivers the Hebrews from Holofernes, she is to be honored for giving her own life for her community (13:20). Although her fame and beauty led to many suitors who desired to marry her, "she remained a widow all the days of her life after . . . her husband died," and died herself at 105 years of age (16:22-23).

The reasons for Judith's role as a model for Christian widows are obvious. She is pious (engages in devotion and fasting); she remains continent (does not remarry); and she actively works in behalf of her community (is not idle, does not "gad about"). Apparently, the problems the pastoral writer faced with the widows were not uncommon to the widows in Philadelphia. The writer's strategy in the longer version of Ignatius's letter is to warn against negative behavior and to provide positive examples.

When Ignatius writes to the town of Smyrna he recalls his encounter with Docetism and elaborates on its dangers to the Christian community. As in *Letter to the Philadelphians,* he stresses submission to the bishop and states that the bishop must be present for a valid Eucharist. In this context, the term "catholic church," *hē katholikē ekklēsia,* appears for the first time in Christian literature; it refers to the universal church in contrast to the local congregation.

Toward the end of the letter Ignatius refers to the hospitality he received during his stay in Smyrna and in his final greeting, he mentions the widows. "I salute the families [or, households] of my brethren with their wives and children, and the maidens who are called widows" (Ign. *Smyrn.* 13.1). This last phrase is sometimes translated, as Schoedel does, "the virgins [*tas parthenou*] who are called widows." The phrase has given rise to a great deal of speculation. Alexander Roberts and James Donaldson suggest that "the *deaconesses* seem to have been called *widows,*"[21] but Ignatius does not mention deaconesses in this correspondence. Cyril C. Richardson admits that the "meaning is not altogether clear. It appears, however, that the order of widows, established for works of charity (cf. 1 Tim. 5:9), sometimes included virgins."[22] McKenna notes that Ignatius in this letter thinks the sixty-year age requirement is being taken lightly.[23] It is difficult

to see how this reading can be deduced from the text. Gryson quotes
scholars who think virgins exercised the same functions as widows,
although he doubts this explanation. He believes Christian virgins
who resolved to remain chaste were called widows and that, like the
widows, the virgins' continence included asceticism, prayer, and acts
of charity, and that, when the virgins were without support, they
were assisted by the community.[24]

While the exact meaning of the phrase "the maidens [or, virgins]
who are called widows" probably cannot be reconstructed, contemporary use of the term *parthenos* and a note on the development of
the "order" of virgins will bring us closer to Ignatius's intent. The
word *parthenos* is best translated "virgin" or "maiden." It is the word
the Septuagint uses for *bethulah* (literally, "separated"), which in the
Hebrew may simply mean a young woman of marriageable age. In
the Septuagint, *parthenos* is used twice for either a marriageable maid-
en or young married woman (cf. Gen. 24:43; Isa. 7:14). It is also
used for a young bride, one's marriageable daughter, and, in a second-
century inscription, for a child of five years of age![25] Discussion of
the use of the term in the New Testament deals primarily with the
mother of Jesus, but the term is also used for the daughters of Philip,
who were prophetesses (*parthenoi prophēteuousai,* Acts 21:9), and for
the young woman in Paul's hypothetical case in 1 Cor. 7:36. The
term is noticeably absent from the pastoral epistles. While there were
apparently always celibates in the church, in New Testament times
they were not an organized body; only in the fourth century do "the
virgins" begin to appear as an order in the church.[26]

Who, then, does Ignatius greet when he greets the "virgins who
are called widows"? Since he salutes them in connection with families
(husbands, wives, children), perhaps he is greeting the young, marriageable women. A more likely possibility is that he is greeting the
young widows who are not enrolled. I have argued earlier that 1
Tim. 5:11-15 discusses a group of young, chaste widows who were
not to be enrolled in the order or numbered with the "true widows."
The pastoral writer encourages them to remarry; thus, this group
would be *parthenoi* in either sense of the Septuagint's use of the term:
it would include young, married women and young women of marriageable age. Because it is not unusual to find in Ignatius's letters
references to the Septuagint and its Greek usage, and because the

reference in question appears in the context of greetings to families, this reading of the phrase has a sound basis. Ignatius greets that group of widows who were not enrolled. They are virgins in the sense of being chaste but also in the sense of being marriageable young widows. If this reading is correct, then *Letter to the Smyrnaeans,* in addition to providing the usual picture of widows as those requiring care (cf. Ign. *Smyrn.* 6.2), suggests that the different categories of widows which we have postulated in 1 Timothy 5 were also functional in other second-century communities.

Ignatius's final reference to the widows occurs in his personal letter to Polycarp, the bishop of Smyrna, who later made a collection of Ignatius's correspondence (Polycarp, *Philippians* 13). This short letter encourages Polycarp in his duties, especially in the care of weaker members of the community, and encourages the community, in turn, to be responsive to its leadership. Little new information about the widows' situation is obtained from this letter. Polycarp is enjoined, "Let the widows not be neglected; after the Lord, you be their guardian" (Schoedel, *Polycarp* 4.1). Because the widows have low social status, they run the risk of being disregarded. It is impossible to say whether or not Ignatius is dealing with the enrolled widows here. Polycarp is to be their protector, the one who thinks of or cares for them, but whether or not this implies an ecclesial relationship is purely speculative. The fact that Ignatius continues, "Let nothing take place without your approval; nor do you do anything without God" is tantalizing. Were some in the community working with widows in a manner unpleasing to its leadership? Were false teachers circulating in the community? Was Polycarp himself expanding or contracting the ranks of the widows? Unfortunately, this letter does not answer these questions.

In summary, Ignatius envisions a chain of command originating with God and proceeding through the bishop to the people. The bishops, then, must take care not to neglect any in their charge. "Ignatius makes it a reproach against certain heretics that they neglected widows . . . and urges Polycarp not to neglect widows, but to make them his especial care."[27] The social position of the widows in the churches he addresses is apparently the same as that held in New Testament communities. Ignatius echoes several of the concerns of the pastoral writer concerning widows, reflects their inclusion in

the church's orders of ministry, and raises the issue of their relation
to a group referred to as "virgins." Ignatius makes it clear that Christian communities must not neglect their widows. Polycarp, by enu-
merating the tasks and attitudes required of widows, gives special
reasons why the widows must not be neglected.

POLYCARP

Polycarp lived from about A.D. 70 to 155/56. His life encompassed
the critical period of the church's development when the apostles and
first missionaries died, and when the "church institutional and orthodox" took shape and faced Docetic and gnostic heresies and growing persecution by Rome. Our earliest account of Polycarp is the letter
from Ignatius to him. Since Ignatius died in the reign of the emperor
Trajan, Polycarp must have been between forty and fifty years old at
that time. His later years are attested by Irenaeus, who probably met
him in Rome before his martyrdom (at which time the good bishop
confessed that he had been a Christian for eighty-six years), and who
reports that Polycarp wrote numerous letters. The only one Irenaeus
cites, and the only one known to Eusebius, is *Polycarp to the Philippians.* Its authenticity is not in question.

Two things seem to have occasioned the letter. First, there was
disorder in the church connected with the behavior of one presbyter,
Valens, and with heresy. Second, the Philippians were apparently
making a collection of Ignatius's letters and wrote to Polycarp for
help with the task. *Polycarp to the Philippians* seems to be a cover letter
for copies of Ignatius's epistles to which Polycarp had access. It is, in
style and tone, simple and direct, and largely devoid of rhetorical
flourishes. The letter indicates that Polycarp knew the Synoptic Gospels and Acts, the Pauline epistles, and 1 Peter, James, and 1 and 2
John. His use of early Christian writings is one of the principal interests of the letter.[28] For our purposes, the letter gives us a glimpse
of a "new kind of status the Christian Church could afford to women,
especially in a place where the Jewish presence was not strong."[29]

Polycarp's advice to the church about widows occurs early in the
letter, in a general section of exhortation. Presumably addressing the
men (husbands), he first reminds them that love of money is the root

of all evil and that the first duty is not to amass wealth but to "teach ourselves to walk in the commandment of the Lord" (Pol. *Phil.* IV.1). The brethren are to teach their "wives to remain in the faith given to them, and in love and purity, tenderly loving their husbands in all truth, and loving all others equally in all chastity, . . . to educate their children in the fear of God" (IV.2).

W. E. Thomas has pointed to several noteworthy features of this "training of wives." First, wives are not to be servants of their husbands but are to take a lively interest in the faith (being knowledgeable enough to teach children). Polycarp enjoins a relationship based on love, not obedience. Furthermore, so long as a wife maintains marital fidelity, she has free social access to the members of the Christian community.[30] To use the terms of the pastoral writer, "gadding about" does not appear to be a problem.

From husbands and wives, Polycarp turns to what the widows are to be taught. These instructions follow the section on family structure, but precede the instructions to the deacons, young men, and presbyters. It is not clear whether the widows should be thought of as appearing with the list of church officials. But this is not too troubling in light of the fact that Polycarp is generally silent on the question of organizational arrangements at Philippi. (The fact that he makes no mention of the monarchical episcopate is a problem that has generated scholarly interest.) Orders of ministry in the church are mentioned in passing only twice, and in neither case is the order the primary issue being addressed. In listing the duties of presbyters, "caring for all the weak" and "neglecting neither widow, nor orphan nor poor" are the first responsibilities mentioned (VI.1).

Turning to the widows, then, we find that they are to be encouraged in two positive ideals: they are to avoid several negative behaviors and to think of themselves as an altar of God.

> Let us teach the widows to be discreet in the faith of the Lord, praying ceaselessly for all men, being far from all slander, evil speaking, false witness, love of money and all evil, knowing that they are an altar of God, and that all offerings are tested, and that nothing escapes him of reasonings or thoughts, or of "the secret things of the heart" (IV.3).

The widows are to be taught two duties: to be discreet in the faith of the Lord, and to pray ceaselessly for all. The term that Lake translates "discreet" (*sōphronousas*) comes from a verb meaning "to be in one's right mind" or "to think sensibly or seriously" (*sōphroneō*). Its adverbial form implies showing self-control or decency. The noun *sōphosynē* is used with this implication in 1 Tim. 2:9: "Women should adorn themselves modestly and sensibly." Interestingly, a similar form appears in Titus 2:2, 5, where young women are exhorted to be "loving to their husbands, to their children, sober minded." Adolf Deissmann has collected a number of examples of the use of *sōphrōn* as an ideal of womanhood. James H. Moulton and George Milligan quote a passage from Gilbert Murray's *Rise of the Greek Epic* in which "with saving thoughts," *sōphrōn saophrōn*, is contrasted with "with destructive thoughts," *olophrōn:*

> There is a way of thinking which destroys and a way which saves. The man or woman who is *sōphrōn* walks among the beauties and perils of the world, feeling the love, joy, anger, and the rest; and through all he has that in his mind which saves. Whom does it save? Not him only, but . . . the whole situation. It saves the imminent evil from coming to be.[31]

That Polycarp uses *sōphronousas* in this context is instructive. First, he has just spoken about wives and children in terms reminiscent of the Pastorals, so the vocabulary of the pastoral writer must have been present in his mind. In fact, in his next phrase he quotes 1 Tim. 5:5. Second, he chooses a term for widows which was, in popular use, an ideal for women (an acceptable, laudatory term in society). Third, the word implies that the widows are to use their minds in a way that will further not only their own spiritual development but the community's as well. Like the men and women whom Murray describes, the widows, through their positive example, change the situations in which they find themselves. They are to be sensible, serious, selfcontrolled "in the faith of the Lord."

Gryson suggests that the " 'faith' . . . which the widows owe to the Lord parallels the 'pledge' " in 1 Tim. 5:12.[32] Earlier we noted that the "first pledge" (1 Tim. 5:12) may refer to an oath of celibacy taken by widows on their enrollment; it was their pledge of constancy in the service of Christ and his Church. If this is the case, then Polycarp is also reminding the widows of the need to be sensible and selfcontrolled in light of (or because of) their pledge to the Lord. The first "duty" then can be interpreted on three levels: *the literal level,* which would call for chaste behavior of any Christian widow; *the public level,* which would ask Christian women to behave in a manner society found praiseworthy; and *the level of the order,* which reminded the widow that her behavior must reflect the pledge she has taken to Christ and that a proper demeanor on her part benefits the whole community.

The widow's second duty is to "pray ceaselessly for all," to plead, appeal, or turn to God on behalf of all Christians. Certainly Polycarp has in mind the ceaseless prayers that 1 Tim. 5:5 demands of the widows. This requirement strengthens the third and most technical reading of the preceding passage, namely, that the widow's tasks fulfill an important function on behalf of and within the Christian community: the widow is the community's example of chaste behavior, and she lifts up its members to God in prayer. Turner remarks that the "primary office of the widows was that not of Martha but of Mary: they 'intercede' . . . for all."[33]

Polycarp next turns his attention to a problem that was discussed in detail in the context of the Pastorals: speech. "Slander, evil speaking, and false witness" are all sins of the tongue. Each causes dissension and thus breaks down the unity of the Christian community.[34] It is also possible that the phrase "evil speaking and false witness" refers to the problems of heresy and false teaching in the community.

That the widows are to shun "love of money and all evil" serves to bring closure to this group of admonitions; it was the reflection with which Polycarp began his instructions to husbands. This directive to widows also recalls the longer text of Ignatius's *Letter to the Philadelphians,* where the widows are warned not to be "fond of dainties." Acute material poverty apparently led some of the widows to covetousness and envy. Not having enough money apparently led them to "love" it for itself. This attitude, which overstepped the bounds set for widows—who had no other means of support—led to injury or harm. The widows must avoid avarice because they are an "altar of God."

Here Polycarp introduces the image that dominates the discussion of the literature of widows: *the widow as altar.* As we shall see, it is of primary importance in our discussion of Tertullian. It appears in the *Didascalia Apostolorum*, the *Apostolic Constitutions*, Methodius's writings, and other Christian works of the second to fifth centuries (Gregory Nazianzus, Pseudo-Ignatius, and *Testamentum Domini*, for example). The changing implications of the image have been discussed at length by scholars who have studied the widows, most notably Carolyn Osiek.[35] Osiek notes that the "origins of the equation widow = altar undoubtedly lie in the early Christian enthusiasm for comparing Christian categories of people to objects and persons from the Old Testament and the idealized time of Jesus."[36] For example, in the *Letter to the Magnesians*, Ignatius compares the bishops to God, the presbyters to the "Council of the Apostles," and the deacons to the "service of Jesus Christ" (Ign. *Magn.* VI.1). Such comparisons are quickly elaborated to include other offices of ministry (deaconesses = Holy Spirit; widows and orphans = altar of burnt offering; virgins = altar of incense). We will discuss these comparisons later.

Here in *Polycarp to the Philippians*, the image of the altar is doubly interesting because the context does not make it clear whether the widow is the altar or the gift laid upon it. The widows are reminded of what they may and may not do because they are God's altar and "everything laid on the altar is inspected with minute and meticulous care. That examination of the offering, ordered by the Jewish law, corresponds to God's searching knowledge of the thoughts and secrets of the hearts of those consecrated to him."[37] Polycarp may have in mind *1 Clem.* XXI.3 ("Nothing escapes [God] of our thoughts or of the devices which we make") and XLI.2 (where the ranks of offices or functions in the church are compared to the offerings brought to the altar to be inspected by the high priest). The question arises, If the widow is the altar, aren't the gifts to be "laid upon" it? "In the older dispensation the offerings which were presented to God were offered and partly consumed upon the great altar of the temple court, but under the new dispensation they are distributed among widows . . . who were in need."[38] Thus the community's offerings for her support would be the offerings that needed examination. It seems, however, that it is the widow's thoughts and motivations that Polycarp feels need to be pure.

How might the widow's service be seen as sacrificial? Lampe gives several examples of the metaphorical use of *thysiastērion* for the process by which the rational soul mortifies the passions, and in which prayer is the offering of sacrifice.[39] These two activities are exactly what Polycarp requires of the widows: providing a faithful example of the chaste life and engaging in prayer. Further, in Rom. 12:1 (and in Ps. 40:6-8) obedience (whether active or passive) to the will of God is a form of sacrifice to God that imitates the obedience of Jesus that led to his being "sacrificed." Certainly it is obedience to the requirements set down by the order which motivates the widows' "discretion," speech, and attitude toward material things. The comparison of the widows to the altar not only reflects "their dedication to God, their mission of prayer for all, and the necessity for them to avoid the defilement of external or internal sin"[40] but it also reflects a life of active sacrifice on behalf of (or for the sake of) the Christian community (see chap. 7 below).

While *Polycarp to the Philippians* does not clearly demarcate the work of the widows, it indicates the qualities of moral and personal integrity that are sought in a woman to be enrolled, and it suggests that she will have a marked responsibility for intercessory prayer. Her importance as the "altar of God" points to her focal position in public worship.[41] Gryson's comments summarize the material in the letter:

> The "faith" . . . which widows owe to the Lord parallels the "pledge" . . . in 1 Timothy 5:12. "Praying unceasingly on behalf of all" recalls 1 Timothy 5:5. . . . Also, "refraining from all slander, gossip, false witness" echoes Titus 2:3 . . . and 1 Timothy 5:13. . . . The idea that widows are the "altar of God" . . . may be understood in two different ways: (1) that widows, who live by the generosity of the faithful, are like altars upon which these gifts are offered to God; or (2) that widows owe uninterrupted prayer to God. . . . Regardless of the exact nature of this connection between the text of Polycarp and 1 Timothy, there is no doubt that the word *chēra* at this time was used as a technical term meaning an ideal life-style, and not merely the fact of being a widow.[42]

SHEPHERD OF HERMAS

According to the Muratorian Canon list, the *Shepherd of Hermas* was written during the time "his brother Pius was sitting on the throne of the church . . . of Rome."[43] So this "apocalypse" must have been written in Rome around A.D. 148. Because its literary genre is that of a series of visions or revelations (five visions, twelve mandates, and ten similitudes), we are wise not to plumb it for reliable historical data. Still, we should note that several of the mandates and similitudes enjoin care for the widows and orphans (Man. 8.10; Sim. 1.8, 5.3.7). *Similitude* 9.27.2 praises particularly the bishops who "ceaselessly sheltered the destitute and the widows by their ministration, and ever behaved with holiness."[44] These bishops who always protected the widows are to be protected by God forever.

The section of the *Shepherd of Hermas* which has the most interest for our study is *Vision* IV.2-3 in which an ancient lady (*hē presbytera*) delivers a book of instructions to the elders. The vision's recipient is to write two books and to "send one to Clement and one to Grapte." With hers, Grapte is to "exhort the widows and orphans."[45] Nothing is known about this Grapte; whether she was herself a widow and the reason for her appointment to this task are not revealed. Gryson suggests that she was a well-known figure like Clement, and that her name is used as a device to give credibility to the writing.[46] We have no supporting evidence that this was the case.

Although Leopold Zscharnack's classic study suggests that the *Shepherd* establishes the existence of a clerical office of widows,[47] it is more responsible to say that the *Shepherd* is not a trustworthy source. We can, at best, suggest that it reflects (as Clement certainly does) the existence of widows in Rome who required assistance and supervision. It also allows for the possibility of a woman in a leadership role with a teaching function, and it suggests that widows were routinely instructed ("Grapte shall exhort [*noutheteō*] the widows").

CONCLUSIONS

The witness of the Apostolic Fathers bolsters the assertion that there "is no single period in the history of the early Church for which evidence of the existence of an order of widows is lacking."[48] Not surprisingly, the view we have of the widows in the second century in Asia does not differ greatly from that in the pastoral epistles. They were an organized group of "pensioners" and, as such, the special concern of the bishop.[49] They were entrusted with the function of intercession in behalf of the community. As the language of Ignatius and Polycarp suggests, they were to be living examples of Christian behavior for the sake of the community. As we have noted, the "comparison of widows to the altar of God reflects their dedication to God, their mission of prayer for all, and the necessity for them to avoid defilement of external or internal sin."[50] This first appearance of the image of the altar is important and will figure significantly in our later discussion of the widows.

While it seems extreme to argue (as Robert Frick does) on the basis of Ignatius and Polycarp that the order of widows gave service by visiting poor, sick, and old women, it is certainly true that the widows were not simply objects of the church's benevolence.[51] In the texts discussed above we see evidence of the various uses of the term "widow" that were delineated in the discussion of the Pastorals. It is evident that the behavior of the widows in orders was strictly regulated and that they were responsible both for active service (intercession) and passive service (attitude and example) in the Christian communities of the second century.

EXCURSUS: EXTRACHURCH SOURCES ON WOMEN IN EARLY CHRISTIANITY

Before we move from the Greek Fathers of the second century to the Latin Fathers of the third, two extra-church sources of information on women in the early church should be noted: *The Epistle of Pliny* the *Younger to Trajan* and Lucian's *Death of Peregrinus.*

Pliny

Early in A.D. 112, Trajan sent the lawyer Pliny to the badly managed province of Pontus-Bithynia on the Black Sea. Pliny's tenth book of letters describes the situation he found. Two of those letters deal with Christians.[52] Apparently the poor state of the temples in Amastris had been blamed on the Christians and, in an attempt to discover the truth of the matter, Pliny detained, tortured, and executed a number of Christians. *Epistle* 96 records,

> So I thought it . . . necessary to inquire into the real truth of the matter by subjecting to torture two female slaves, who were called deacons; but I found nothing more than a perverse superstition which went beyond all bounds.[53]

The letter gives us important information about women in church office. First, the deaconesses mentioned in 1 Tim. 3:11 had survived and were functioning as a recognizable group within the Christian community. Both orders for women that originated in apostolic times—widows and deaconesses—had survived into the second century.[54] Second, apparently neither low social status nor sex ruled out the possibility of holding office in the church. In fact, as in apostolic times, many Christians were slaves, and in Acts women were often the first in communities to accept the gospel. While the letter does not give direct information on the function of deaconesses in the Christian community, it indicates that they were prominent enough to be recognized, seized, and martyred.

Lucian

Lucian of Samosata records that the pagan philosopher Peregrinus (d. A.D. 165) had converted to Christianity while in Palestine and had subsequently been imprisoned for this decision. When his release was not secured, the Christians surrounded him with all sorts of attention. From morning until night the widows and orphans stood before the jail. "Old hags, 'widows' they call them, and orphan children took up their position outside the gaol: Christian officials made a night of it with him . . . and holy prayers of theirs were recited."[55]

While nothing definite should be concluded from the passage if for no other reason than that Lucian is a hostile witness in regard to Christianity, the passage does suggest that the widows were a special group within the community and that visiting prisoners, or at the very least holding prayer vigils in their behalf, was part of their work. 1 Timothy required enrolled widows to have raised children. Since they were often mentioned in conjunction with orphans, it is tempting to suggest that the widows Lucian encountered were responsible for the care and nurture, if not the material support, of the orphans mentioned with them. Certainly the uncomplimentary designation "old hags" corroborates that sixty years of age was a requirement for enrollment. Apparently none of the younger widows attended Peregrinus!

Even if Lucian "as an outsider, knew [Christianity's] doctrines and institutions only superficially,"[56] that alone would serve to underline the prominence, or at least visibility, of the widows in the Christian community.

Neither of the sources mentioned in this short digression can be used as hard evidence in the case for an active order of widows (or women generally) in the second-century church. It is, however, noteworthy that even pagan writers, who would have had little interest in the church's structure of leadership, were aware of Christian women in visible public roles. The student or scholar who carefully surveys these sources might well turn up, even in passing references, important information that would advance our understanding of the fascinating and shadowy issue of official roles for women in the second-century church.

5

Tertullian
of Carthage

INTRODUCTION

Some church historians have traced the development of early Christianity in terms of triads of cities.[1] During the apostolic period, Jerusalem, Caesarea, and Antioch led the advance of Christianity. Then, from A.D. 70 to 170 missionary activity centered around Antioch, Ephesus, and Rome. When we reach the third century, Rome, Carthage, and Alexandria become the leading cities of Christendom. As we move from the Apostolic Fathers to Tertullian and the earlier apologists of the Old Catholic period, along with the developing church, we move geographically from Europe and Asia Minor to Africa.

Christianity may have arrived in North Africa from Rome—there was always a close connection between Carthage and Rome—but what led to its expansion there is uncertain. Frend speculates that the expansion may have had something to do with the Roman attempt to standardize the traditional cults in Carthage. In any case, the history of the church in Africa begins when the proconsul in Carthage condemned the Christians of Scilli to martyrdom on August 1 in the year 180.[2]

The African church was from the beginning a church of martyrs, characterized by a "spirit of desperation and contempt of death"[3] and an unwillingness to compromise with "the world." Septimius Severus continued persecution of the Christians, and Jews, in 202–3. The prison diaries of Vibia Perpetua provide firsthand information about the church in Carthage at this time. If her reflections are typical, the church was filled with apocalyptic hopes and felt itself under the direction of the Holy Spirit.[4] Tertullian's adage that the church flowers from the blood of its martyrs is verified by the third-century church in Africa.

In spite of persecution, an early third-century council of North African bishops presided over by Agrippinus, bishop of Carthage, had seventy in attendance. In the period in which the larger church achieved a canon of Scripture, rules of faith, and a well-argued defense against Gnosticism, Africa was the "teacher of the entire Christian Church in the west."[5] This is the world into which Tertullian came.

Tertullian appears in the midst of a flourishing church in Carthage, a city second only to Rome as a cultural center. The verb "appears" is used advisedly; the dates used in connection with Tertullian are entirely conjectural. He was born the son of a centurion in the service of civil authorities in Carthage between 145 and 160. Educated in Rome, he made a reputation for himself as a jurist (which in no small measure accounts for his style as a writer). He apparently was not converted to Christianity until he returned to Carthage around 185. Jerome reports that Tertullian was a presbyter in Carthage, though Tertullian makes no mention of his clerical status in his writing, which covers the period from 195 to 220. After 220 there is no knowledge of him.

Tertullian is known primarily for the essays and polemics that helped to establish Latin (rather than Greek) as the ecclesiastical language in the West. The "creator of ecclesiastical Latin,"[6] he wrote short sentences that were parallel in form and antithetic in content. A master of style and language, he was well suited to be the apologist for Christianity to the pagan world. Most of his works are occasional and are written to discuss the relationship of Christians to heathens. In each of the works an opponent, who is made out to be clearly in the wrong, is attacked and beaten. Tertullian marshals all the powers of rhetoric to win his argument. In addition to regulating Christians' relations to the pagans around them, Tertullian writes about church life and discipline and enters into dogmatic controversy, although he is primarily a moralist, not a philosopher. His essays are usually classified as pre- or post-Montanist.

Since the nineteenth century it has been argued that we must see Tertullian as the founder of western Christianity and not primarily as a Montanist.[7] However, because it is common knowledge that Tertullian became a Montanist early in the third century (c. 207),

and because of the prominent role of women in the Montanist movement, a short description of that sect is in order.

As we noted earlier, there was conflict in the church from the
beginning between those who encouraged efforts to regularize church
order and its clergy, and persons who wanted to allow charismatics
with spiritual gifts the free operation of those gifts. In some ways,
Montanism is another instance of this tension between "office" and
"gift"; it pitted the bishop against the prophet.

Montanism arose in the middle of the second century in isolated
regions of Asia Minor. In the village of Ardabace, on the border of
Mysia and Phrygia, a newly baptized convert, Montanus, fell into an
ecstasy and declared himself to be the prophet of the Holy Spirit. Two
female disciples, Prisca and Maximilla, also claimed this gift. Word
spread quickly of this new, enthusiastic form of prophecy and its
"final" revelation from God. Montanists saw in their prophets the
fulfillment of John's promise of the Paraclete. If in Christianity the
dispensation of the Father had given way to the dispensation of the
Son, then in Montanism both gave way to the dispensation of the
Spirit.[8]

The basic content of Montanist prophecy was twofold. First, the
end of the world was imminent, as evidenced by wars and rebellions.
Second, the holy city of Jerusalem was to descend from heaven, where
Christ had appeared as a shining female figure. On the basis of the
Montanists' belief in an immediate apocalypse, they taught that marriage was an earthly bond preventing full consecration to God and
they advised against new or second marriages. In addition to celibacy,
the ascetic practices of Montanism included fasting and a generalized
contempt for things of "the world." Because of this tendency, Montanism opposed the kingdoms of this world and it met persecution
with defiance. Because Montanism ruled out flight in the face of
persecution, some have suggested that its adherents sought martyrdom.

The movement spread rapidly, especially in Roman Africa, where
Tertullian encountered it. Frend notes that because it became the
religion of Christian peasantry, Montanism produced the first social
and religious schism of the Christian East.[9] Montanism, however, had
its own troubles, as persons in addition to the original three prophets

claimed the prophetic gift and thus called into question the authenticity of the New Prophecy. While it lingered on, and we find scattered references to it until the fifth century, the movement as a major force died out about two hundred years after its founding.[10]

It should not surprise us that a moralist like Tertullian became a Montanist. His writing indicates that he understood himself morally to be reborn through Christianity. He describes the difference between a pagan and a Christian life, and in his essays his opponents' points of view tend to spring from what Tertullian indicates is a lack of morals. It is understandable that he would embrace a movement that encouraged the kind of moral strenuousness evidenced by requiring women to be veiled, forbidding second marriages, and having inflexibly hard attitudes toward backsliders. The church itself became Tertullian's worldly opponent when it would have nothing to do with the New Prophecy.

We are now in a position to discuss the widows in the third-century church. It was during this time that the widows reached their highest official position in the hierarchy of the church. Tertullian clearly refers to them as an order in the "Exhortation to Chastity." As we shall see shortly, he was concerned with the status of the widows; he saw them as a distinct group taking precedence over others, and he discussed the requirements and obligations of the order. The primary sources of information about the widows are found in Tertullian's "On the Veiling of Virgins," "Exhortation to Chastity," and "To His Wife." The three works are dated between 204 and 207, approximately the time Tertullian became a Montanist.

"ON THE VEILING OF VIRGINS"

Tertullian argues that it "behooves our virgins to be veiled from the time that they have passed the turning-point of their age."[11] His principal argument for veiling is drawn from 1 Cor. 11:5-16, which begins, "Any woman who prays or prophesies with her head unveiled dishonors her head—it is the same as if her head were shaven." Paul indicates that veiling is a mark of servitude in Christian worship (vv. 7-9). "The unveiled woman dishonours her head, because that is the part in which the indecency is manifested. Also by claiming equality with the other sex she disgraces the head of her own sex."[12]

Paul apparently has married women chiefly in mind in Corinthians, and he appeals on the basis of established custom. In Ramsay's classic work, *The Cities of St. Paul*, the oriental view is explained rather quaintly:

> In Oriental lands the veil is the power and the honour and dignity of the woman. With the veil on her head, she can go anywhere in security and profound respect. She is not seen; it is the mark of thoroughly bad manners to observe a veiled woman in the street. She is alone. . . .
> But without the veil the woman is a thing of nought, whom anyone may insult. . . . A woman's authority and dignity vanish along with the all-covering veil that she discards. That is the Oriental view, which Paul learned in Tarsus.[13]

Three points need to be considered when reading Tertullian. First, he does not seem to comprehend the obvious fact that Paul admits that women, as a matter of course, pray and prophesy in public worship.[14] In "On the Veiling of Virgins," Tertullian categorically declares, "It is not permitted to a woman to speak in church."[15] This injunction is odd if "On the Veiling of Virgins" is a Montanist text. We have described the role played by women in that sect, especially by Maximilla and Prisca, whose oracles Tertullian quoted at least twice[16] (once, as we shall see, in connection with the widows).

Second, Tertullian apparently argues that virgins as well as married women are to be veiled, though this is a complicated matter (as the amount of space devoted to it in chapters 5, 8, 9, 11, and 17 of the essay suggests). Third, while Paul appeals to the common custom of his time, Tertullian seems to be asking for a return to a practice that has passed out of fashion. He begins, "This observance is exacted by truth, on which no one can impose prescription—no space of times, no influence of persons, no privilege of regions. . . . Our Lord Christ has surnamed Himself Truth, not Custom."[17] While the veil was customary for women in the East, and those women going about without it were subject to serious misjudgment, the ancient Egyptian, Ethiopian, and Greek women, as well as inhabitants of Asia Minor, were not veiled.[18] Alexandria would certainly have been influenced by Egyptian and Ethiopian practice, and the women of Carthage, already under Rome's cultural dominance, may have been free of the veil.

The section of Tertullian's essay germane to our inquiry is chapter 9, subtitled by Roberts and Donaldson "Veiling Consistent with the

Other Rules of Discipline Observed by Virgins and Women in General." The information it reveals about the widows occurs in an outburst against an instance in which a teen-age virgin has been numbered with the widows. Tertullian's outrage at such a practice indicates that several of the conclusions we drew about the order of widows in our study of 1 Tim. 5:3-15 (chap. 3 above) hold for the widows Tertullian was acquainted with. Furthermore, we learn of the widows' pastoral duties and of the practice of giving them special seating in the congregation.

Tertullian begins, "I know plainly, that in a certain place a virgin of less than twenty years of age has been placed *in the order of widows!*"[19] Clearly, in Tertullian's churches the widows are an order with age as the primary condition for enrollment. Later in the passage, Tertullian explicitly quotes the sixty-year age requirement. Tertullian continues, "If the bishop had been bound to accord her any relief, he might . . . have done it in some other way without detriment to the respect due to discipline."[20] The young woman in question might well have fallen into the group we termed the young widows of 1 Tim. 5:11-15. Although they were too young to qualify for the order, they were not to be excluded from aid if it were necessary. We cannot imagine, however, that Tertullian would agree with the advice that these young widows remarry.

Of the other requirements for enrollment with the "true widows," Tertullian enumerates "single-husbanded," "mothers," "educators of children," "in order that their experimental training . . . may . . . have rendered them capable of readily aiding all others with counsel and comfort, and . . . they may . . . have travelled down the whole course of probation whereby a *female* can be tested."[21] Apparently the widows Tertullian was acquainted with were called upon to perform pastoral duties ("counsel and comfort"). Having already passed through the trials attendant to married women, their age both gives them the experience for counseling and assures the church that they are trustworthy and will uphold its moral standing in the larger community. And, of course, the widow is now free to do such work.

The implication of a pastoral office changes the picture heretofore drawn of the widows' responsibilities in the church. We also find the suggestion that they were afforded special, honorary seating in the congregation. In upbraiding the bishop who would enroll a teenage

widow, Tertullian writes, "The authority which licenses her sitting
in that seat *uncovered* is the same which allows her to sit there as a
virgin: a seat to which (besides the 'sixty years') not merely 'single-
husbanded' . . . are at length elected."[22] That this seating is with the
clergy is attested by another of Tertullian's essays, "On Monogamy,"
in chapter 11: "With what face do you request (the solemnizing of)
a matrimony which is unlawful to those of whom you request it; of
a monogamist bishop, of presbyters and deacons bound by the same
solemn engagement, of widows whose Order you have in your own
person refused?"[23]

Commenting on this text Gryson notes, "All scholars . . . affirm
without any reservation that Tertullian ranked the widows among
the clergy. . . . This official position appears concretely in the fact that
widows occupied a place apart in the assemblies of the community."[24]
Tertullian's treatise "On Modesty" records that penitents seeking rec-
onciliation were to prostrate themselves before the widows and presbyters. "Introducing into the church . . . the repentant adulterer, lead
into the midst and prostrate him, all in haircloth and ashes, . . . before
the widows, before the elder, suing for the tears of all."[25] The widows
who "sit in front" in the Egyptian community "are assisted by the
Church but as part of the clergy engaged in ministry, and not simply
because of poverty."[26]

In Tertullian, we have the first allusion to a practice that apparently
became standard: seating the widows with the clergy. In the fourth
century, the *Apostolic Constitutions* give evidence of the practice: "Let
the virgins, and the widows, and the elder women, stand or sit before
all the rest."[27] By the writing of the *Testamentum Domini* (in the latter
half of the fifth century, in Syria) the verb "seated before," *proka-
thēmenai,* is almost synonymous with "widows," who are assigned
almost all women's ministry.[28] Furthermore, at least some archaeological evidence indicates that churches were changed structurally to
accommodate the increased numbers of clergy. For example, the front
of the magnificent fifth-century basilica at Kourion in Cyprus was
extended, the new and extended walls visibly encompassing the old.
Just beyond the altar of the basilica was a crescent of masonry supporting a partition that separated the sanctuary from the apse at the
east end. "Initially, the bishop's throne would have been set against
this partition. Later, the partition was enlarged into a platform to

carry the throne (possibly with benches for other clergy on either side). . . . Such alterations were imposed by changes in ritual during the long period . . . which the cathedral served the city."[29] Perhaps, as the practice of seating the widows "at the front" reached Cyprus, the basilica was altered to make room for them.[30] Admittedly this is speculation.

Returning to the literary evidence, we noted earlier that Ignatius of Antioch mentioned "virgins called widows." Our careful exploration of the Greek revealed that he may not, in fact, have reflected a practice that Tertullian clearly felt was an abuse. Tertullian states that "on the ground of her position, nothing in the way of public honor is permitted to a *virgin.*"[31] Tertullian's point in chapter 9 of "On the Veiling of Virgins" is that if the bishop in question had to provide for the needs of a very young widow, he could have done so in ways other than by enrolling her in an order for which there were, first, clear conditions for admission, and second, important pastoral responsibilities that she was too young to discharge properly.

"EXHORTATION TO CHASTITY"

Probably written about the same time as "On the Veiling of Virgins," the "Exhortation to Chastity" urges rejection of this "necessity of the flesh" on the basis of God's will and God's "image," that is, the person of Jesus. Chastity may be from biological birth, from spiritual birth at baptism (including, by mutual consent, married persons), from widowhood, or "after renunciation of sexual connection" in marriage.[32] Much of the exhortation (seven of thirteen chapters in Roberts and Donaldson's edition) argues against polygamy and second marriages. "Renounce we things carnal, that we may at length bear fruits spiritual" neatly summarizes Tertullian's argument.[33] He insists that one gains the Spirit by "parsimony of the flesh" and quotes the Montanist prophetess Prisca to prove that the carnal nature dulls the spiritual faculties.[34]

In chapter 10, Tertullian seems to insist that the advantage of continent widowhood is heightened spiritual perceptivity. Tertullian, however, is not unaware of the "excuses by which we colour our insatiable carnal appetite." Among those excuses are numbered "props to lean on," households to manage, families to be governed, and domestic duties to be looked after.[35] Tertullian dismisses these excuses by raising a series of ironic questions. Apparently alluding to Paul's suggestion that Cephas traveled with his wife (1 Cor. 9:5), Tertullian writes,

> Why moreover, Christian, are you so conditioned, that you cannot (so travel) without a wife? "In my present (widowed) state, too, a consort in domestic works is necessary." (Then) take some spiritual wife. Take to yourself from among the widows one fair in faith, dowered with poverty, sealed with age. You will (thus) make a good marriage. A plurality of *such* wives is pleasing to God.[36]

A man unable to look after his own domestic affairs is to choose from the order of widows a woman meeting all the qualifications for the order (performing good works, being without means of support, being over sixty years of age) to be a "spiritual wife," that is, to be his housekeeper but not his bedfellow.[37] A number of such wives is pleasing presumably not only because such marriages are asexual but because they diminish the number of women the church must support in the order.

Jo Ann McNamara's essay "Wives and Widows in Early Christian Thought," though otherwise a very helpful article, is misleading in its analysis of Tertullian's advice here. The chaste marriage, she says, provides a means "of disposing of the women who had been induced by ascetic principles to stand alone in the world but who had not the means to support that ambition."[38] While it is true that the means of self-support for unattached and unprotected women was severely limited, this is not the group to whom Tertullian alludes in chapter 12. He speaks of women possessing the qualifications for the order; by definition, they thus had a means of support in the order.

Tertullian's use of the term "order" here (*ordo,* or "in the *ordines*") is borrowed from Roman institutions. In closing his exhortation, he refers explicitly to the widows as an order. "How many men, therefore, and how many women in Ecclesiastical Orders, owe their position to continence, who have preferred to be wedded to God."[39] The women in the orders of the church must certainly be the widows, who, like male members of the hierarchy, were to have been married only once, and were not to remarry (cf. chapter 8 of Tertullian's essay and 1 Tim. 3:1-13).[40] In Tertullian we find proof of the ecclesiastical order of widows: the widows clearly appear alongside male clergy in seating and function in "On the Veiling of Virgins" and "On Monogamy"; and they are explicitly called an *ordo* (with qualifications alluded to) in "Exhortation to Chastity." Before concluding our study of Tertullian by looking at his advice in "To His Wife," we must acquaint ourselves with the ascetic tendencies in early Christianity in general.

EXCURSUS: ASCETIC TENDENCIES IN EARLY CHRISTIANITY

In some ways the increasing concern with sexual renunciation in early Christianity simply reflects the preoccupation of the non-Christian world with continence. In Cynic and Stoic diatribe we find the ideal of the detached "wise man." In Neoplatonism, where the first step toward perfection is to subdue the body, asceticism reached its highest point.[41] The Jews, on the other hand, saw fecundity as a special mark of God's favor. "Both Jews and Romans assumed that women would spend their lives as married persons who, if widowed or divorced, would marry again with as little delay as possible. A woman who failed to enter a new union would remain under the authority and protection of her father, her in-laws, her sons, or a guardian designated by one of them."[42]

The Christian community, however, tended from its beginning to have a special regard for celibacy. This could have been influenced by the example of Jesus himself, or by association with groups like the Essenes, who abandoned traditional social expectations in light of their apocalyptic hopes. While Peter may not have been the only married apostle, the silence of Scripture on this point indicates that it was a matter of indifference.[43] References to continence and virginity abound in the New Testament (see Matt. 19:11, 12, 29; 1 Cor. 7:7-9, 32-34). Paul saw marriage primarily as a lawful way to channel the lusts of the flesh.

By the second century, Christians were beginning to refuse the social requirement to marry and have children. We see in Christian tracts a renewed emphasis on celibacy, virginity, and abstinence from sexual intercourse, with an additional stress on the undesirability, indeed sometimes the illegitimacy, of second marriages.[44] As mentioned earlier, Augustus had attempted to eliminate celibacy by law. "He sought to have everyone married all the time, at least until they had reached the age where procreation was unlikely. Widowed and divorced persons were to be rushed into new marriages."[45] Augustinian law was refined and promulgated by later Roman emperors, and just thirteen years before Constantine rescinded them, such laws were praised as the "foundations of the state: they have always furnished a seedbed of youth to the Roman armies, bearing the fruit of human bodies."[46]

Christians apparently viewed family life as they viewed the state—as a necessary evil. The expectation of an immediate end to the physical world

and its institutions led Christians, who in the second century had attempted
to conform to the empire, to march with apparent unconcern into a threat-
ening social conflict.[47] "Christian concern for the individual over the family,
their disdain for the traditional power of fathers and husbands and their
indifference to procreation were not the least reasons why the religion continued to be persecuted for three centuries."[48] Virginity became second only
to martyrdom in the hierarchy of merit, and the connection between the two
has not been fully plumbed by scholarship. In disregard of Roman law, the
most common form of Christian asceticism was the practice of voluntary
continence by both sexes. The conflict between Roman law and Christian
practice was a serious problem until Constantine abolished the last of the
Augustinian laws, thereby making celibacy no longer a crime. (It is noteworthy that the community of virgins experienced its greatest growth after
the Constantinian Edict of 313.)[49]

This sketch gives an impression of the effect sexual asceticism had on the
relations between Christianity and the Roman Empire. What was its effect
within the Christian community? Succinctly stated, "the Christian ideal of
virginity offered a unique autonomy to women who abdicated their fundamental social responsibilities."[50] Several recent studies on the Apocryphal
Acts have remarked on the importance of this fact. Written for Christian
audiences or as conversion propaganda (by communities of continent wom-
en, according to Davies),[51] the legends of the Apocryphal Acts follow a general
pattern involving the conversion of a woman whose mate is of high social
standing in the community that the apostle enters. The wife is converted to
Christianity and accepts a sexually continent life. Virtually all the stories
contain a motif of erotic substitution; the Christian teacher is substituted for
the mate, who opposes and then punishes the newly converted wife. In the
Apocryphal Acts, Christianity is defined as the acceptance of an ascetic way
of life.[52]

Kraemer and Davies have argued that the Christian message appealed to
women who were previously defined only in relation to men and to marriage.
Severance from family life had certain positive effects for these women. In
an essay on sexual equality and the cult of virginity in early Christianity, Jo
Ann McNamara writes,

> From best to worst, marriage is a state of bondage from which the only
> escape is celibacy. . . . Praises of the virginal state were not the result of
> an attitude antithetical to sexual relations in themselves. . . . Nor did
> they proceed from enmity toward women. . . . Virginity was presented
> as an ideal higher state for all and, practically considered, as an oppor-
> tunity to obtain freedom from that condition which alone defined the
> inferior status of the female.
>
> At the very least, the virgin woman could expect release from the
> governance of a husband and the chains of children. She was free of the
> burden of worldly cares and responsibilities that weighed her sisters
> down.[53]

Unmarried women enjoyed greater freedom for instructional and intellectual efforts than their married Christian sisters. Furthermore, activities the church would not have countenanced by married women were not only tolerated but also praised when performed by celibates. Celibacy offered to women "who would have been hidden in domestic life, novel personal liberty."[54] As we have seen, the widows in particular gained a measure of personal liberty when, by their vow to the order, they were placed outside the authority structure of the family. The first to institutionalize celibacy, the widows were the first women to achieve autonomous status in the Christian community.

Not surprisingly, the widow's autonomous status led to conflict within the community. "Having broken free from legal and social bondage to marriage, widows would not have wanted to place themselves in a position of complete and unquestioning subservience to the male church hierarchy."[55] As we trace the development of the order we shall see that the very positions on sexual continence and widowhood (and the condemnation of second marriages) that were considered not only orthodox but also exemplary led women into positions that were condemned by the writers who advocated them in the first place!

In the case of Tertullian, the very way of life he advocated served to liberate women from the roles to which he would have liked to limit them. It is ironic that the writer who so strongly condemned the Marcionites advocated the life-style that liberated women to behave in ways he disapproved of and felt to be characteristic of the Marcionite heresy.[56] This historical paradox—that sexual continence both liberated women (and the widows) and opened them to severe criticism by the major voices of orthodoxy—should be kept in mind as we review Tertullian's "To His Wife."

"TO HIS WIFE"

Tertullian addresses this argument against second marriages to his "best beloved fellow-servant in the Lord" because he has thought it wise "to provide for the course which you must pursue after my departure from the world." His provision for her is to give "the counsel of (perpetual) widowhood." While marriage is good, celibacy is better, and in any case at the resurrection there will be "no resumption of voluptuous disgrace between us."[57] "To widowhood signed and sealed before the Lord nought is necessary but perseverance."[58]

Tertullian again catalogues and refutes the arguments for second marriages, but asks his wife not to believe herself unable to function without a man's protection, guidance, and leadership. Nor does he believe that a man requires a wife to care for his household.[59] Heathens, he argues in chapter 4, abstain from second marriages to honor beloved husbands.[60] Continence "has been pointed out by the Lord of salvation as an instrument for attaining eternity, and as a testimony of (our) faith."[61] Second marriages are thus detrimental to faith:

> How detrimental to faith, how obstructive to holiness, second marriages are, the discipline of the Church and the prescription of the apostle declare, when he suffers not men twice married to preside . . . when he would not grant a widow admittance into the order unless she had been "the wife of one man"; for it behooves God's altar to be set forth pure. That whole halo which encircles the Church is represented (as consisting) of holiness. Priesthood is (a function) of widowhood and of celibacies among the nations.[62]

Once again, Tertullian clearly refers to the widows as an order and asserts his belief that this is the reality to which 1 Tim. 5:9, 10 refers. "The apostle declares, when he suffers not men twice married to preside, when a widow is not admitted to the order unless 'the wife of one man.' "[63] The reason for this prohibition is, again, that God's altar must be pure. The aura surrounding the church must be one of holiness, and that holiness is assured by sexual purity.

S. Thelwall's translation (in Roberts and Donaldson) of the next line is misleading. He translates "Priesthood is (a function) of widowhood and of celibacies among the nations.[64] *Sacerdotium viduitatis, et celebratum est apud nationes* might be more accurately rendered, "Priesthood (nominative) (is) of widowhood, and is celebrated among nations." "Priesthood" is in the nominative case and "widowhood" (or "of the widowed") is in the genitive. I suggest that Tertullian is referring to his argument in chapter 6 that even heathens commend widowhood and celibacy. The intriguing turn of phrase is *Sacerdotium viduitatis*. While it would be tempting to suggest a priestly function for the widows, it would be irresponsible on the basis of the text alone to see their ministry of prayer and teaching as intercessory in a priestly sense. The point Tertullian makes is that all church officials must be sexually pure, either chaste or married only once (1 Tim. 3:2, 12).[65]

Tertullian believes the death of a husband is God's way of calling the widow to continence. "Tertullian denied that he was simply seeking to exercise exclusive possession of his wife since resumption of their sexual union was inconceivable in that other world. . . . Rather, he was speaking from genuine love in urging her to take advantage of the opportunity for more perfect blessings."[66] He closes book 1 of "To His Wife" by discussing the honors the widow enjoys in God's sight; specifically, she is God's special concern and is on a par with her benefactors. She is ranked above the virgins because "it is easy not to crave after that which you know not, and to turn away from what you have never had to regret."[67] There are, however, dangers attendant upon widowhood. A widow must not be a "wanderer," and she must remember that "talkative, idle, winebibbing, curious tent-fellows, do the very greatest hurt to the purpose of widowhood."[68] Talkativeness leads to immodesty; idleness seduces from strictness; winebibbing encourages evil; and curiosity conveys a spirit of rivalry and lust. Tertullian warns against the very pitfalls the pastoral writer enumerated.

Having argued eloquently against second marriages and for the sanctity and honor of widowhood in book 1 and, thus, for the value of that order, Tertullian then softens his position in book 2. All he asks is that, should his wife choose to remarry, she marry a Christian. Marrying "in the Lord" is permissible even if it is not, in Tertullian's mind (or in the apostle Paul's), the most advisable course of action. Although Tertullian is drawn to sexual asceticism, he stops short of completely condemning the flesh and its sexuality, which, in the final analysis, God created.

In "To His Wife" Tertullian gives the following information about widows: they are honored by the Christian community as an example of bodily purity; and they are an order in the same category as those who preside over churches. The widows are again imaged as God's altar, and it is suggested that they sanctify the gifts of their benefactors. Because they are honored by and serve as examples to the community, they must avoid "gadding about," idle talk, and drunkenness. In short, we see a remarkable continuity with the widows of the Pastorals, but now the certainty of an order is perfectly clear.

CONCLUSIONS

The brief citations we have examined from Tertullian indicate that even at the beginning of the third century, the era of their greatest influence, the widows were prominent. Zscharnack's classic turn-of-the-century study on women in early Christianity cites Tertullian as the source for the assertion that the only women in orders in the first

half of the third century were the widows.[69] The information Tertullian provides about the order at this time is remarkably consistent
with the view we have in the pastoral epistles of the New Testament.
Enrolled widows were to be over sixty years of age, financially dependent, married only once, and possessed of mature life experience.
They were warned against second marriages (which would prohibit
enrollment), purposeless wandering about, idle talk, and drunkenness. In agreement with the Apostolic Fathers, Tertullian insists on
the sexual purity of the widows and uses the metaphor of the altar
of God in connection with them.

In addition, Tertullian tells us that the widows in early-third-cen-
tury Carthage (and perhaps in Rome, where he had lived)[70] were
definitely an order (*ordo*), and he, with the pastoral writer, lists them
with bishops, presbyters, and deacons. This grouping is also attested
in Syria around A.D. 200 by Pseudo-Clementine and by Clement of
Alexandria.[71] Their clerical status and the general public approval that
they receive from the community are apparent in the fact that the
widows are seated with the clergy. With this honor come the responsibilities of pastoral duties, specifically "counsel and comfort."

Tertullian was heavily influenced by the sexual attitudes of Christianity in his era, especially by the Montanists, who reasoned that
since there was no marriage in heaven, and since the end time was
imminent, marriage was an unnecessary encumbrance. Still, one can
hardly agree with Cadoux, who glibly calls Tertullian a woman hat-
er.[72]

Tertullian tells his wife she need not submit herself to the protection
and authority of a man. Nor does he see women primarily as do-
mestics and housekeepers. Tertullian, of course, was not aware of the
long-term implications of these assertions, nor of the social effect
within the Christian community of the freedom that widowhood gave
to Christian women. To give credit where credit is due, however,
Tertullian's willingness to allow an official status for women in the
church is certainly admirable.

We must also admit that the order of widows was probably a necessity, and an institution inherited by Tertullian's church. In the
evolution of the church's ministry, Zscharnack sees the order of widows as a bridge between office and charism.[73] Certainly in the case

of Montanism it is easy to see how charismatic gifts could get out of hand. Developmentally, then, McKenna is correct: "The definite official status bestowed on the widow in the third century was probably an attempt to institutionalize the charismatic, didactic rights of the prophetesses."[74]

6

The Widows in
the Third Century

INTRODUCTION

The situations of the church and the empire in the latter half of the third century are in some ways parallel: both are in crisis. Schaff calls this second period of Christianity the Age of Persecution; others refer to this time period as one of "imperial crisis and recovery."[1]

Early in the century, the prosperity of the empire was at its peak. In the East the growth of cities was fortified by commerce. By A.D. 250, however, we see the disruption of the imperial system. The emperor was drawn solely from the ranks of the army. The imperial army lacked discipline, and this further weakened the system of central authority. In 251 the Goths invaded the Balkans, and Decius became the first emperor to be killed by barbarians. Serious threats to the empire continued until Diocletian (284–305) transformed arbitrary army rule into a new system of government, a tetrarchy in which each front had a sort of mini-emperor. Ruling with Maximinian, Diocletian secured the boundaries of the empire and tried without much success to raise its economic level.

In 305, however, Diocletian and Maximinian were forced to abdicate. Leadership fluctuated until 312, when Constantine the Great earned his epithet at the battle of the Milvian Bridge outside Rome.[2] Under Constantine the empire was divided into East and West. This led to the rise of the East and the decline of Rome (especially after Egyptian corn was directed to Constantinople rather than to Rome). Constantine's impact on the development of Christianity is well known, and we shall allude to it later. For now, we will examine the condition of the church during the time the empire was besieged with problems.

The church was, in short, not much better off than the empire. The crisis between church and state has been succinctly analyzed: Each emperor was supposed to bring a golden age of peace. Worship of the emperor, therefore, was the political policy of patriotic conservatives.[3] To intensify the cult of the emperor, in 249 Decius called for a universal act of sacrifice. When Christians refused to comply, persecutions began in earnest. From December 249 to February 250 the force of the empire was directed against Christian leaders; the bishop of Rome, Lucins, was imprisoned and murdered in 250. In the summer and fall of 250, subjects of the empire were required to sacrifice to the emperor. Porphyry, hardly a lover of Christians, reports that a thousand Christians were put to death for their refusal to apostatize. The letters of Cyprian from 248 to 258 give the same grim picture of the church in Africa. Historians note that this call for sacrifice was political and not religious. Unity in the empire was needed at the time of the barbarian invasions. Still, Christians paid the price in blood for the emperor's ineffectualness.

The situation did not improve under Valerian. In 257 he launched a new campaign of persecution intended to turn popular indignation against the Christians and to divert attention from himself after a series of military defeats. Again, he began with the arrest of the church's leaders. In August of 258, Roman bishops, presbyters, and deacons were scheduled for execution. The persecution ended only when Valerian was taken by the Persians in 260.

The last quarter of the century saw persecution gradually diminish. By 300 there were senior officers in the army who were Christians, and there were Christians at the emperor's court. But the spirit of Diocletian's reforms was religious-conservative. What is now referred to as the Great Persecution[4] began in Nicomedia in February 303, when an edict against Christians was posted. The Christian who tore down the edict was reportedly roasted alive. This was a portent of things to come.

Church property was seized by the empire; church buildings were razed, and the Scriptures were burned. Upper-class Christians lost their privileges, and all Christians lost legal protection. Clergy were incarcerated and often killed. Eusebius writes,

> We saw with our very eyes the houses of prayer cast down to their foundations . . . and the inspired and sacred Scriptures committed to the

flames in the midst of the market-places, and the pastors of the churches
. . . were ignominiously captured and made a mockery by their enemies.[5]

Christians were compelled to make sacrifices to the emperor, and
those who refused were subjected to acts of torture so grisly as to
raise the ire of a generation of us inured to such horror by a steady
stream of blood from the television. Eusebius writes as an eyewitness
that the corpses of those who died were refused burial and fed to
beasts. In Leitzmann's words, however, "the heroism of the few won
the victory."[6] In April 311 Galerius published an edict that put to an
end the official persecution of Christians. This was followed by Constantine's Edict of Toleration at Milan.

As we look at the position of women and of the widows in the
third century, we must keep these historical backdrops in mind: the
instability of the empire and the violent persecution of Christians and
the church.

WOMEN AND WIDOWS: AN OVERVIEW

Several historians note the prominence of women and widows in
the third century. Cadoux writes, "Women filled an important and
recognized place in the life of the Christian community." He believes
they performed limited ecclesiastical duties and that the restrictions
placed on them were not so much intended to limit women as to
prevent scandal in the larger community.[7] The prominence of women
is confirmed in Eusebius's accounts of the persecutions. One is struck
by the number of women whose martyrdoms are recounted and wonders if "that marvellous aged virgin Apollonia," or "Mercuria, an
aged woman of reverend mien," or Dionysia and Ammonarion ("a
holy virgin" and "true champion") were members of the order of
widows.[8] All were put to death.

McKenna concurs that the position of the widows reached its highest point in the third century, when the widows were clearly listed
as an official part of the church hierarchy.[9] Both Clement of Alexandria and Origen place the widows in their hierarchies,[10] indicating
something of their position in the East. And, as we noted earlier,
Cornelius's letter to Bishop Fabian of Antioch (c. 250) states that
there were more than fifteen hundred widows in Rome.

Gryson devotes an entire chapter to the Alexandrian Fathers of the third century in *The Ministry of Women in the Early Church*.[11] Rather than replicating good work, I shall summarize it here.

Gryson notes that Clement (150–215) and Origen (185–254) included the widows with the bishops, presbyters, and deacons. In general, both Clement and Origen give instructions to the widows which follow those laid down in the pastoral epistles. They especially stress the prohibition against second marriages and insist that the only teaching function of the widows is in connection with the training of young women, to inculcate in them the "qualities which make them good wives, good mothers, good housekeepers, gracious and charitable Christians."[12]

Gryson devotes much attention to Origen's references to "washed the feet of the saints," one of the requirements in 1 Timothy 5 for an enrolled widow. In Origen's *Commentary on John* the spiritual interpretation of this gesture is discussed in connection with Jesus, who asked the disciples to repeat the action. Origen concludes that this demand in 1 Timothy should not be understood literally: "Do not hesitate to interpret symbolically the expression, 'washed the saints' feet,' since senior women just as senior men, are ordered to be the 'teachers of good things.' "[13] Origen understood that to wash the feet of someone meant "to purify the blemishes of his soul with fitting words."[14] In the text of his sixth homily on Isaiah, Origen writes,

> If you wish to understand more clearly how the widow "washes the feet of the saints," listen to Paul, who . . . commands widows "to teach what is good, and in such a way that the young women may remain chaste," thus washing the stain off the feet of the young women. And these widows are worthy to be honored in the Church who wash the feet of the saints through spiritual instruction—by saints I mean not men, but women. For: "I permit no woman to teach or to have authority over men." He wants women "to teach what is good" in the sense that they have to inculcate chastity in "young women," not young men, for it is not becoming for a woman to be a teacher of men; but they must train young women in chastity and love of their husbands and of their children.[15]

While admitting that the women teach, Origen insists that their teaching should be addressed only to women. In a comment on 1 Cor. 14:34-35 he insists,

"For it is improper for a woman to speak in an assembly," no matter
what she says, even if she says admirable things, or even saintly things,
that is of little consequence, since they come from the mouth of a woman.
"A woman in an assembly": clearly this abuse is denounced as improper—an abuse for which the entire assembly is responsible.[16]

In response to the prominence of prophetesses in Montanism, Origen
asserts that under no circumstance may a woman (enrolled widow
or not) speak in an assembly where men are present.

Gryson's treatment of the Alexandrians, especially of Origen, is
enlightening. We must, however, part company with his conclusions.
He suggests that while both Clement and Origen recognized that
women (especially deacons) served the church in Paul's time, they
do not suggest that this office survived. Similarly, Gryson says that
when Clement lists the widows among the number of "chosen people," and Origen notes their preeminence in the church (they were
granted ecclesiastical dignity just as bishops, presbyters, and deacons
were), they are dealing with "theoretical considerations, not with
references to a concrete situation and a living practice."[17] If the widows (or deaconesses) were not part of a "living practice," why was
Origen so concerned to see that they teach only other women? Why
give such vehement instructions if no women were "speaking out of
turn"? Why devote so much attention to a dead institution? Why,
in the *Commentary on the Epistle to the Romans,* would Origen exhort
the senior women to train the younger women[18] if this were not of
concrete, existential concern to the church in Egypt? It seems that
Danielou—who maintains that in the third century widows were an
order in the Egyptian church and were understood to be part of the
ecclesiastical hierarchy—is more nearly correct. Certainly this conclusion would be more in line with another branch of the church in
the East which we know by the evidence provided in the Syrian
Didascalia Apostolorum, which gives an extended treatment of the widows.

DIDASCALIA APOSTOLORUM

The *Didascalia Apostolorum* (hereafter *DA;* see n. 25 below) is the
most instructive text we have on the widows in the third century. It
is a church order modeled on the *Didache* (Teaching). It dates from
the first decade of the third century and probably originated in north-
ern Syria.[19] Written in Greek (except for a fragment of book 3) the

DA survives only in a fourth-century Syriac version, although important fragments (including some dealing with the widows) of a late fourth-century Latin version exist. The *DA* is apparently a source for the first six books of the *Apostolic Constitutions* (c. 370),[20] and some scholars believe that in sections where the two works agree, the original Greek of the *DA* is preserved.[21] Gryson has noted that the *DA* "reveals in an exceedingly lively way what the widows stood for in a Syrian community in the first half of the third century."[22] The work gives regulations for and admonitions to the widows, and "principally aims at moral instruction."[23]

First, as in earlier lists in which church officials are compared to temple furnishings or heavenly orders (especially the Epistles of Ignatius, specifically *Mag.* IV), in the *DA* the widows appear with bishops, deacons, presbyters, and here, deaconesses:[24]

> The bishop sits for you in the place of God Almighty. But the deacon stands in the place of Christ; and do you love him. And the deaconess shall be honoured by you in the place of the Holy Spirit; and the presbyters shall be to you in the likeness of the Apostles; and the orphans and widows shall be reckoned by you in the likeness of the altar.[25]

The author chooses an image for the widows which was already used by Polycarp—*the altar* (see chap. 7 below). In passing, we note that in liturgical assemblies where the faithful were grouped by rank, the widows had their own place.[26]

Chapter 14 of the *DA* deals with the appointment of widows and makes it clear that no widow under fifty years of age may join the order lest she later marry and cause scandal, or take the church's charity and then marry, thus depleting the church's resources.[27] The editor of this edition of *DA* notes that there was definitely an "order," although the age of fifty may have been the only absolute qualification for membership.[28] Young widows were not to be admitted to the order for the aforementioned reasons, but they, like the orphans, were eligible for support if they had no other source of income. Support was indirect; charitable donations were made to the bishop, who distributed them at his own discretion.[29] Apparently, if a widow were over fifty but had means of support, she was not eligible for the order. Thus there were two classes of widows, the enrolled and the unenrolled. Hereafter, we shall discuss only the enrolled widows.

Like the pastoral writer and the Apostolic Fathers, the writer of the

DA is at pains to preserve the church's resources. But the many instructions to the bishops concerning the widows indicate that the writer is also concerned for the spiritual well-being of the community. As noted, support for widows was indirect. The bishop was to distribute gifts to the widows, and to tell the widows who their benefactors were so that they could pray for them. The transaction was a spiritual one. One of the bishop's major responsibilities, therefore, was to see that gifts to widows came from an honorable source:

> Do you the bishops and deacons be constant therefore in the ministry of the altar of Christ—we mean the widows and the orphans—so that with all care and with all diligence you make it your endeavour to search out concerning the things that are given, (and to learn) of what manner is the conversation of him, or of her, who gives for the nourishment . . . of 'the altar'. For when widows are nourished from (the fruits of) righteous labour, they will offer a holy and acceptable ministry before Almighty God.[30]

Gifts are to be refused from the rich who behave cruelly or oppressively, from the lewd, evildoers, forgers, painters, murderers, idolaters, extortioners, dishonest persons, hypocritical lawyers, dishonest businessmen, and those who practice usury. For if the widow

> be nourished from (the proceeds) of iniquity, she cannot offer her ministry and her intercession with purity before God. . . . For if widows pray for fornicators and transgressors through your blindness, and be not heard, not receiving their requests, you will perforce bring blasphemy upon the word through your evil management, as though God were not good and ready to give.[31]

The fear of the writer is that if widows pray for evil persons unknowingly, and their prayers are therefore not answered, they will lose faith in the goodness and generosity of God. Thus the bishop must heed that he "minister not to the altar . . . of God out of the ministrations of transgression"[32] but instead supply only good gifts, or even himself "invite widows to suppers . . . whom he knows to be in . . . distress."[33]

As in earlier stages of the order's development, the enrolled members have certain duties to perform and a certain deportment to maintain. Now, however, the duties are more extensive than at any prior time; they include obedience, prayer, "good works," making clothes in their homes for those in distress, and visiting and laying hands on the sick, as well as fasting and praying for them. The widows are strictly forbidden to teach or to baptize. The strength of the admonition suggests that some of the widows must have been doing both. The *DA* enjoins widows to be obedient to those listed above them in the hierarchy, especially to the bishop,[34] without whose permission they are forbidden to visit homes, to eat or drink, fast, receive gifts, lay on hands, or pray.[35] In short, the bishop exercises control over the practice of the widows' ministries.

The primary duty of the widows in the *DA* is prayer for the whole church and for their benefactors.[36] They are not to gad about spreading gossip and scandal but to "sit beneath the roof of their houses and pray and entreat the Lord."[37] We shall turn to the "running about" later; here we note that the primary duty of the widow is prayer. As the writer explains, "If two shall agree together, and shall ask concerning anything . . . it shall be given them."[38] Therefore,

> a widow who wishes to please God sits at home and meditates upon the Lord day and night, and without ceasing at all times offers intercession and prays with purity before the Lord. And she receives whatever she asks, because her whole mind is set upon this.[39]

Clearly the writer considers the widow's prayer particularly potent. This is because God's ears are especially attuned to the prayers of the helpless and the lowly and of those whose hearts are set entirely on God.

Although the widows' primary duty is to pray in their homes, they are also called upon to serve actively the church community with good works; "for if one practise good works, she shall be praised and accepted."[40] Visiting and ministering to the sick and "working at wool" are the widows' principal works.

The widows are enjoined to visit the sick (and not to feign sickness themselves!) rather than calling on those able to make large donations to the church. A widow's supplications at the bedside of the sick are particularly valued, especially when linked with fasting and imposition of hands.[41] (One wonders if they are welcome also for their practical experience and wisdom about treatments or home remedies for various illnesses.) Gryson observes that when the writer of the *DA* insists that widows are to bless and not to curse, he is probably referring to this gesture of blessing.[42] If this is the case, then the

widows exercise a function that is later to be appropriated solely for
the ordained priesthood. It is little wonder then that the church wants
the widows' visitations strictly regulated by the bishop.

The second good work of the widows concerns the deportment
required of those in the order. The widow is not to be greedy; she is
to stay at home and "works at (her) wool" to provide for others.[43]
Charles C. Ryrie interprets this to mean that she makes garments at
home for those in distress.[44] His suggestion is supported by the story
of Dorcas (Tabitha) in Acts 9:36-43, who made "robes and other
clothing" for the poor widows. The writer of the *DA* notes that when
an enrolled widow thus attempts to provide for others, she is like the
widow who put in a mite.[45] That is, in her poverty she puts in what
little she has, and is therefore to be commended highly (cf. Mark
12:41-44 and parallels). Here, as in other instances, the widow provides the community with dramatic examples of proper spiritual behavior.

The widows of the *DA* obviously have more active ministries than
their sisters in the order at earlier stages and in other locations. The
writer is adamant, however, that they must neither teach nor baptize:

> It is neither right nor necessary . . . that women should be teachers, and
> especially concerning the name of Christ and the redemption of His
> passion. For you have not been appointed to this, O women, and es-
> pecially widows, that you should teach, but that you should pray and
> entreat the Lord God. For [Jesus] . . . sent us the Twelve to instruct the
> people . . . and there were with us women disciples . . . but He did not
> send them to instruct the people with us. For if it were required that
> women should teach, our Master Himself would have commanded these
> to give instruction with us.[46]

Whatever we may think about the author's interpretation of the Gospel accounts, his position is manifest. Furthermore, "teaching" is very
strictly understood. If a widow is questioned about the Christian faith,
she is only allowed to reply to the most rudimentary issues. For
example, she may speak against idols or of the unity of God, but she
is not to answer questions about the incarnation or passion of Christ
or about eschatology. Her duty in such a situation would be to refer
the questioner to church leaders (men) for instruction.[47] The writer
clearly believes both that the widows are incompetent to teach and
that unbelievers would not take seriously teaching, or even opinions,

of old women. Apparently, any information communicated by the widows would fall into the category of old wives' tales. The right to baptize was also expressly forbidden to widows:

> That a woman should baptize, or that one should be baptized by a woman, we do not counsel, for it is a transgression of the commandment, and a great peril to her who baptizes and to him who is baptized. For if it were lawful to be baptized by a woman, our Lord . . . would have been baptized by Mary His mother. . . . Do not therefore imperil yourselves, brethren and sisters, by acting beside the law of the Gospel.[48]

The issue comes up because, apparently, some widows either dared to baptize or claimed for themselves and their order the right to do so. While in these matters the author reflects a disdain for women which characterized the mindset of his age, it is also noteworthy that he denies women in general, and the widows in particular, the right to teach and to baptize, because he did not find precedent in the Gospels for either. We cannot exaggerate the influence that the cultural setting had on the author's thought; the same argument is used today to limit the extent of women's service to the church.

The writer of the *DA* clearly shares with the pastoral writer, the Apostolic Fathers, and Tertullian a concern for the position of the church and Christians in the society at large. This concern leads him to include a chapter on "how widows ought to deport themselves."[49] "Every widow . . ought to be meek and quiet and gentle."[50] She should avoid causing scandal by spreading gossip from house to house. She must be neither greedy for herself nor jealous of another widow's good fortune in receiving gifts. "Those who are gadabouts and without shame . . . are no widows, but 'wallets,' and they care for nothing else but to be making ready to receive."[51] This untranslatable play on words (*non viduae, sed viduli*) suggests that their "God was their wallet; they turned their state of life into a business."[52] Obviously such examples of bad deportment would harm the Christian cause and reflect badly on the church.

In this regard, that which the author bars the widows from doing and the negative behavior he chastises are as informative as the instructions he gives for admission to the order and for its duties. The primary shortcomings the widows were susceptible to were, in the writer's experience, "running around," greed, envy, and "questioning."

The writer deals extensively with the problem of "gadabouts." Because the widow is the altar of God, she should remain stationary. Those who run about are characterized as "gossips and chatterers and murmurers, they stir up quarrels; and they are bold and shameless." Moreover, "by their chattering they execute the desires of the Enemy."[53] The writer is obviously concerned that the widows will spread gossip, thereby creating dissension and malice within the Christian community. Satan is understood to be using the old tactic of "divide and conquer."

The prohibition against widows teaching may also offer a clue to the problem being addressed. In the pastoral epistles, younger widows were barred from the order because, among other things, the writer felt they might spread false teaching in the course of their daily rounds.[54] In that context, gadding about was equated with straying after Satan (1 Tim. 5:13-15). Here in the *DA*, the fear may be that by gadding about in unrestricted visitation (that which was not for the official purpose of ministering to the sick), the widows in orders might be tempted to teach or to answer questions about the faith, thereby performing functions denied them by the bishop.

Furthermore, unlimited visitation was potentially a source of disruption within the order. The writer of the *DA* felt that one reason the widows ran about was that they were greedy to receive things.[55] Not only was greed unbecoming to any Christian woman but its first cousin, envy, threatened the harmony of the order:

> Now we see and hear that there are widows in whom there is envy one toward another. For when thy fellow aged woman has been clothed, or has received somewhat from some one, thou oughtest, O widow, on seeing thy sister refreshed . . . to say: "Blessed be God, who hath refreshed my fellow aged woman," and to praise God; and afterwards (to praise) him that ministered.[56]

If the widow stays at home praying and "working at her wool," she is less likely to compare her state with that of her sisters, and, thus, there is no opportunity for the seeds of jealousy and envy to be planted.

Finally, the widows should not gad about, because it leads them to "ask questions." "But now we hear that there are widows who . . . care only for this, that they may stray and run about asking questions."[57] One translation of the *DA* suggests that "ask" may mean "beg."[58] If this were the case, then the church would be disgraced, for the widows would be giving public evidence of the church's inability to care for its own. The widows would prove there were "needy ones among them" (Acts 4:34-35). But on the basis of the context, and of the way the *Apostolic Constitutions* renders the section, it seems unlikely that "beg" is the sense intended here. It is not entirely clear what sort of questions the widows are raising. Are they making inquiry of a doctrinal nature? Are they questioning the authority of the bishop or others over them?

The context suggests that some of the widows are trying to find out who has given alms for their support:

> She who has received alms of the Lord—being without sense, in that she discloses (the matter) to her that asks her—has revealed and declared the name of the giver; and the other, hearing it, murmurs and finds fault with the bishop who has dispensed.[59]

The widows are expressly told to suppress the name of any benefactor, "that his righteousness may be with God and not with men."[60] Secrecy in these matters is important both to prevent dissension and envy in the church community and to prevent the church's private business from becoming public. The writer imagines the church as the right hand and the heathens as the left; one is not to know what the other is doing (cf. Matt. 6:3-4).

In concluding the survey of the prohibitions and warnings against negative behavior which the writer of the *DA* addresses to the widows, two things are especially noteworthy. First, in almost every instance the reason for the prohibitions and warnings is, at least in part, the spiritual well-being either of the widows themselves or of the church. The writer's interest may be more than to limit the order of widows; the intention may be to provide the best conditions possible (as he understands them) for the spiritual development of the whole church.

Second, the image of *the altar* often appears in the course of the writer's admonitions. The widow is not to "run around," because she is the altar of God and must stay in one place.[61] Widows who are "running after gain; and . . . chattering" do "not conform to the altar of Christ."[62] It is because she is "the holy altar of God, (even of) Jesus Christ" that the widow must not divulge the name of her benefactor.[63] The bishops are to be constant "in the ministry of the altar of Christ—we mean the widows and the orphans" to be sure "the nourishment . . . of 'the altar' " comes from appropriate sources.[64]

In its original use in the *DA*, the widow as altar appears in a clerical list of correspondences which explains the clergy.[65] Its use in connection with admonitions, however, follows Polycarp's "Letter to the Philippians" (IV); the widows are an "altar of God, and . . . all offerings are tested."[66] That is, both the altar and the gifts laid on it must be pure. Furthermore, the altar is understood to be stationary and, therefore, reinforces the limitations on the widows' movements; they are to remain in one place because the altar does. Osiek believes this use of the image reflects growing limitations on the order.[67]

CONCLUSIONS

In the Christian literature of the third-century church, the widows hold a prominent place. They are consistently listed with the clergy. As members of the church hierarchy, the widows are targets of the persecutions of the age, as Eusebius reports. Clement of Alexandria and Origen give instructions for the widows similar to those in the pastoral epistles. Origen allows the widows a teaching function, although he strictly limits the privilege.

The *DA* gives us the most information on the widows in the third century. As in earlier times, they are the special concern of the bishop; they are to be fifty years of age for enrollment; and they are to be supported by indirect donations channeled through the bishop. In return for the support they receive, the widows "are to spend their time in prayer, . . . should work at wool to give to those in distress and should visit the sick, laying their hands on them and praying with them."[68] Gadding about, gossiping, envying, and questioning are to be strictly avoided. The widows are not to baptize or teach (the need for a prohibition suggests that some, in fact, did so). The writer of the *DA* is at pains in his instructions to the widows to preserve the church's financial resources and its standing in the general community, but he also reflects a concern for the spiritual well-being both of the widows and of the church. As Gryson concludes,

> Widowhood appears in the *Didascalia* as a privileged opportunity for spiritual progress. Accentuating the ascetic features of the "real widow" in First Timothy, the author neatly draws the outlines of a spiritual ideal

composed of two essentials—continence and prayer. For widows over fifty, agreement with this ideal was sanctioned by entering the "order of widows."[69]

It is worth noting that James MacKinnon detects in the writer of the *DA* a marked distrust of the widows.[70] Both MacKinnon and McKenna believe that the charismatic spirit of ministry has survived into the third century in the widows and their supporters, and that the object of the writer is to stamp out what remains of this spirit in the community, or at least to institutionalize it.[71] The influence of the widows is curbed by the rise of the deaconesses, who are close associates of the bishop in pastoral work.

Gradually the rich vocation of the official widow passes to the clerical deaconess. We see in the *DA* the beginning of the ascendancy of the deaconess over the widow. The widows are not to teach. The deaconesses, however, teach newly baptized women. A century later, the *Apostolic Constitutions,* although borrowing from the *DA,* shows the near complete decline of the order. In that work the widows are subject to deaconesses, who administered their sustenance.[72]

7

The Widow as Altar:
Metaphor and Ministry

As we have seen, a great many issues in church history and feminist theology are raised by examining the history of the widows. In concluding this study, we will confine our attention to one image that has appeared throughout the early literature: *the widow as the altar of God*. It occurred first in Polycarp's epistle "To the Philippians." "Let us teach the widows to be discreet in the faith of the Lord . . . knowing they are an altar of God, and that all offerings are tested, and that nothing escapes him of reasonings or thoughts, or of 'the secret things of the heart' " (IV.3). The passage assumed the widows to be a recognizable group whose primary function was intercession. The metaphor "an altar of God" and the statement that the offering is tested are noteworthy since they suggest, in addition to biblical allusions to the altar of sacrifice and to 1 Tim. 5:5, the necessity for multiple functions within the church.

A generation later, the image turns up in the instructions Tertullian wrote to his wife. In his discussion of second marriages, which are held to be obstructive to holiness, we read that "it behooves God's altar to be set forth pure." [1] Again, the metaphor refers to 1 Tim. 5:9-10 and suggests the need for purity.

In the *Didascalia Apostolorum*, and in the *Apostolic Constitutions*, which parallel and expand it, the widows appear with the metaphor of the altar. Early in the *DA*, in the list of clerical offices we find, "And the orphans and widows shall be reckoned by you in the likeness of the altar." [2] In chapter 1, on the deportment of widows, the author instructs, "But let a widow know that she is the altar of God; and let her sit ever at home, and not stray or run about among the houses of the faithful to receive. For the altar of God never strays or runs about anywhere, but is fixed in one place."[3] The widow who is a gadabout "does not conform to the altar of Christ."[4]

The widows are to pray for their benefactors but not to reveal their benefactors' names. "But do thou in praying for him suppress his name; and so shalt thou fulfill that which is written, thou and the widows who are such (as thou): for you are the holy altar of God, (even of) Jesus Christ."[5] Bishops are to be careful that the benefactors are worthy persons so that the widow's intercessions will be heard. If the widow prays for persons in sin, she will draw the Lord's attention to them:

> Wherefore, O bishops, fly and avoid such ministrations; for it is written: There shall not go up upon the altar of the Lord (that which cometh) of the price of a dog, or of the hire of a harlot. . . .
> Take good heed therefore that you minister not to the altar of God out of the ministrations of transgressions.[6]

The references to widows in the *Apostolic Constitutions* (which is outside the frame of this study because it is much later) largely follow those in the *DA,* although the widows and orphans are "esteemed as representing the altar of burnt offering," and the virgins are "honored as representing the altar of incense, and the incense itself."[7]

Perhaps the *Constitutions* have borrowed this image of the fixtures of the temple from Methodius's *Banquet of the Ten Virgins.*[8] In discourse 5 ("Thallousa"), chapter 8, the writer speaks of the double altar of widows and virgins. If the tabernacle is taken for a type of the church, he reasons, "it is fitting that the altars should signify some of the things in the church." He then compares the brazen altar to the company and circuit of widows, "for they are a living altar of God, to which they bring calves and tithes, and free-will offerings, as a sacrifice to the Lord."[9] The virgins represent the golden altar, so both in the *Constitutions* and in Methodius the beginnings of a shift of focus away from the widows to other groups of women, or perhaps to a general restriction of women's roles in the church, is evident.[10]

The interpretation of the image of the altar has been as follows: "The widows are called the 'altar of God' because they were supported out of the gifts brought to the church at the assembly for worship."[11] They are the altar on which the offerings were piled.[12] In these interpretations, the role of the widow is passive; she receives the gifts of the community. This was, in fact, the case; all the literature on the widows deals with their reception of alms. Still, if we omit later sources like the *Apostolic Constitutions* that clearly list duties performed by the widows, this understanding of the altar image is too narrow.

First of all, the metaphor functions differently in different texts. In each source, the reference is to the altar as the place of sacrifice. Thus, it can be used to discourage "gadding about" in the later sources. In the *Didascalia Apostolorum, Apostolic Constitutions,* and Methodius, it is used to suggest a comparison between church officials and either elements in temple worship or the Trinity and the apostles. Both Polycarp and Tertullian use the comparison to insist on the widows' purity (seen as sexual continence).

But the reference to the altar itself changes. In Polycarp, the widows are "an altar," implying others; in Tertullian, they are "God's altar." The *DA* refers to "the altar," "the altar of Christ," and "the holy altar of God." In Methodius, the widows are a "living altar." It would seem not only that metaphorically the widow is the place of sacrifice, but that she herself performs some active role. If this is true, historians who insist that the widows were just "on the dole" must rethink their position.

When the image is understood, the widow emerges again, as she has throughout this study, as a figure with a positive contribution, indeed, with spiritual power in the Christian community.

THE ALTAR AND THE SACRIFICE

Behind the image of the altar in early Christian literature stood the literal altars in the temple. After the destruction of the temple in A.D. 70, prayer became a legitimate substitute for sacrifice. The precentor in the synagogue was the substitute for the sacrificing priest in the temple.[13] Not surprisingly, prayer in place of sacrifice became normative for Christianity. The Epistle to the Hebrews enjoins, "Let us continually offer up a sacrifice of praise to God, that is, the fruit of lips that acknowledge his name" (Heb. 13:15). The *Didache* refers to the Eucharist and its prayers as "sacrifice."[14]

Those who lift up their voices in prayer are referred to as altars. Clement of Alexandria writes, "The altar . . . is the congregation of those who devote themselves to prayers."[15] In addressing Celsus's remark that Christians "shrink from raising altars, statues, and temples," Origen responds, "We regard the spirit of every good man as an altar from which arises an incense . . . the prayers arising from a good conscience."[16]

By analogy, the widow in her work of intercession was an active, "living altar." She was to continue "in supplications and prayers night and day" (1 Tim. 5:5) and to pray ceaselessly for all (Polycarp, *Phil.* 4.3). Her prayers for the community were especially powerful because God has promised to hear the cries of the widows (see Exod. 22:23; Deut. 10:18).

There is another way in which the widow as altar reflects an active role in the Christian community. To understand it, we must work back to the New Testament from Polycarp. In Polycarp, the image occurs in a section Lake calls "Exhortations to Virtue." Polycarp encourages the Philippian Christian men to arm themselves with righteousness and to teach themselves the commandments of the Lord. The Christian wives are to be faithful, to love their husbands, and to educate their children in fear of God. Next come the instructions about widows which were quoted above. Lake comments,

It has been suggested the image of the altar here refers to *1 Clement* 41.2: Not in every place . . . are the daily sacrifices offered or the free-will offerings . . . but before the shrine, at the altar, and the offering is first inspected by the High Priest and the ministers.[17]

Clement's reference is clearly to the altar in the temple. This is the passage later writers may have in mind when they use the image of the altar to argue that widows should stay at home. Perhaps Polycarp uses it in reference to the testing of offerings. I do not think he had the temple altar in mind. Clement refers to *the* altar *to thysiastērion* Polycarp to *an* altar—the Greek has no definite article. An anatharous noun can be used to describe a quality; it does not necessarily refer to a "thing" (see, e.g., Mark 15:39, which uses an anatharous noun to describe the quality of a person). Here the widow is altarlike.

In commenting on the letter La Porte suggests that the "comparison of widows to the altar of God reflects their dedication to God, their mission of prayer for all, and the necessity for them to avoid defilement."[18] In a short study of the place of women in Philippi, W. E. Thomas notes that widows were marked by the qualities of moral and personal integrity and had responsibility for intercessory prayer. The importance of the "altar of God," however, was its focal point in public worship.[19] Thomas points beyond the "living altar" of intercessory prayer to a greater significance.

Not surprisingly, the majority of the allusions in Polycarp are to the New Testament. Certainly his passage on widows evokes the New Testament in the instruction that the widows are to pray ceaselessly (cf. 1 Thess. 5:17; 1 Tim. 5:5) and in the assertion that God knows the secrets of the heart (1 Cor. 14:25). When we examine the use of "altar," *thysiastērion,* in the New Testament, we find it refers most frequently to the physical altar before the temple.[20]

One of the New Testament uses of "altar" raises an interesting question for our consideration. In the midst of the "woes" in Matthew 23, Jesus asks, "For which is greater, the gift, or the altar that makes the gift sacred?" (Matt. 23:19). Jesus is not making direct reference to cult but has chosen a neat illustration to expose shallow, scribal teaching.[21] And yet the statement implies that the altar is in some way active; it "purifies" the offering.

The link connecting the "activity" of the altar that is implied in Matt. 23:19 and the widows can be deduced from Heb. 13:10: "We have an altar from which those who serve the tent have no right to eat." I suggest that the Hebrew Christians to whom the letter is addressed may have been reproached for having no altar. The reply is that the Christian altar is more adequate than that of burnt offering. F. F. Bruce writes,

> Earlier in the letter the sacrifice of Jesus has been portrayed in terms of the sin offering of the Day of Atonement: his offering, by contrast with the earlier one, is permanently efficacious. There was no literal altar in his case; the term "altar" is used here by metonymy for his self-oblation and the benefits which it secures to believers.[22]

It seems to me that Bruce is correct in his interpretation of Heb. 13:10 and that "altar" is used for "sacrifice."

"Altar," *thysiastērion,* is associated linguistically with "sacrifice," *thysia.*[23] Furthermore, Jesus introduces a new way of thinking about sacrifice. He quotes Hos. 6:6, "I desire mercy and not sacrifice." The scribe who understands Jesus' teaching admits, "To love [God] with all the heart, and with all the understanding, and with all the strength, and to love one's neighbor as oneself, is much more than whole burnt offerings and sacrifices" (Mark 12:33). When Paul pleads with the Ephesians, "Be imitators of God as beloved children. And walk in love, as Christ loved us and gave himself up for us, a fragrant offering and sacrifice to God" (Eph. 5:1-2), he has in mind sacrifice as active love of God manifested in self-giving love of neighbor. The sacrifice is no longer a pigeon or a bull, but oneself, the whole of one's life: "Present your bodies as living sacrifice, holy and acceptable to God, which is your spiritual worship" (Rom. 12:1; see also Ps. 40:6-8). An individual's obedience to God is a form of sacrifice offered to God in imitation of Christ's sacrifice.

It is in this sense that the widow as altar becomes an effective agent; she too is a living sacrifice. The key New Testament texts on widows (Mark 12:41-44; Luke 2:36-38; 4:25-26; 7:11-17; 18:1-8; Acts 6:1-7; 16:11-15; 1 Tim. 5:3-16) do not explicitly connect widows with sacrifice. If, however, love of God, love of neighbor more than self, and prayer are Christian sacrifices, then the widows embody Christian sacrifice. Anna worships "with fasting and prayer night and day" (Luke 2:37). The widow who makes an offering at the treasury exhibits love of God and care for neighbor above self, especially since the offering is her "whole living" (Matt. 12:41-44). It is noteworthy that both these widows are placed within the temple environs, near the altars.

The widow was an effective agent in a spiritual transaction within the Christian community. First, she interceded for the community. Her prayers perhaps sanctified the gifts brought to her. Second, the example of her life of sacrifice provided the community with a living reminder of their Lord's sacrifice. In the words of Saint Basil, the altar is for the purpose of the holy remembrance of Christ in which Christ comes near himself as a sacrifice.[24] Christ provides the atonement through his sacrifice; the altar reminds Christians of his sacrifice (Heb. 13:10). The widow, by her way of life, is an example of (to paraphrase the *Book of Common Prayer*) Christ's "one full, perfect, and sufficient sacrifice" (see Hebrews 5:8-10).

Both 1 Timothy and Polycarp enumerate specific aspects of the widow's example. To be enrolled, a widow must have well-attested good deeds of hospitality and service to the afflicted and must have raised children (1 Tim. 5:10). After she is enrolled, she presumably continues such a life-style, "being far from all slander, evil speaking, false witness, love of money, and all evil" (Polycarp *Phil.* 4.3). Furthermore, the widow is to have "washed the feet of the saints" (1

Tim. 5:10). The image certainly comes from John 13:1-17, where
Jesus stoops to wash the disciples' feet. (Recall Origen's long discussion of foot washing in connection with the widows.) Here are the
practical applications of the theoretical injunctions in 1 Peter 2:5: "Be
yourselves built into a spiritual house . . . to offer spiritual sacrifices
acceptable to God through Jesus Christ." The widows' way of life
embodies exhortations such as "Do not neglect to do good and to
share what you have, for such sacrifices are pleasing to God" (Heb.
13:16).

The widow is required to have been the wife of one husband (1
Tim. 5:9), to be "left alone" (1 Tim. 5:5), and to remain continent
after she is enrolled. Younger widows are not to be enrolled, because
they "grow wanton against Christ" and "desire to marry" (1 Tim.
5:11). In the decision to enroll, a widow presents her body as a living
sacrifice. (See the discussion on asceticism in connection with Tertullian, chap. 5 above.)

Glancing back at the widows in the Gospels and Acts we find that
Anna lived alone without a husband for a number of years. The Greek
text is unclear; it could mean Anna had been a widow for eighty-
four years. She remained in the temple (stationary like the altar?)
and prayed and worshiped constantly (Luke 2:36-38). The women
who accompanied Jesus and the Twelve provided for the men from
their own resources; they did good deeds by sharing what they had
(Luke 8:1-3). Tabitha, probably herself a widow, "was full of good
works and acts of charity" and made coats and other garments for
the less fortunate widows (Acts 9:36-41).

It is interesting that Tabitha made coats, outer garments, because
in addition to being used as clothing, these are what the poor slept
in at night. Deuteronomy commands, "You shall not pervert justice
due to the sojourner or to the fatherless, or take a widow's garment
in pledge" (24:17). Here, too, is one of the tasks that the *DA* gives
to widows: to work at wool. Tabitha's sacrifice was to live unselfishly
and to share what she had. She was more than fulfilling the requirements set down in the pastoral epistles: "Honor widows who are real
widows. . . . If any believing woman has relatives who are widows,
let her assist them; let the church not be burdened, so that it may
assist those who are real widows" (1 Tim. 5:3, 16).

The stories of these widows were preserved by the early church (which seems to have left out so much about the lives and witnesses of women) at least in part because they were "living sacrifices"; they were doing what Jesus had set as the example of, and what the Pastorals had stressed as fundamental to Christian living. The widows were doers of the word, and not hearers only.

We have noted that expositors of the sociology of the pastoral epistles stress that the writer was concerned about what those outside the Christian community might think of it. The writer's concern was that women not give outsiders the opportunity to blaspheme Christianity. This pressure from outside, it is argued, led to a change in the structure of the Christian community. Social pressure caused the church "to move from a *communitas* structure challenging society's norms to a patriarchal structure embracing them."[25] Unfortunately for the church, these analyses appear to be accurate. But there is an even darker dimension at work in the constriction of the role that the widows—and other women—played in the developing church. If we have read the biblical and early literary witnesses correctly, the widows were providing a positive spiritual example.[26] How embarrassing for the male leaders of the Christian communities when those who had the least were continually called upon to do the most! It was so embarrassing that it finally had to be stopped.

Epilogue

The order of widows survived well into the period of the imperial church. Its existence is attested by the great church orders of that period, especially by the *Testamentum Domini* (c. A.D. 350), which gives prayers for the widows' institution, and by the *Apostolic Constitutions* (c. 370). But as we have noted, by the latter part of the third century, the deaconesses' star was ascendant. Although the deaconesses were unknown in the West until the fifth century, they came into being as an order between 200 and 250 and took over the special ministries to women.[1] While there was, for a time, a close relationship between the widows and the deaconesses, it was the deaconesses who eventually assumed the duties of visiting the poor, instructing women, and assisting at their baptisms. Some indication of the shifting fortunes of the widows' order is evident in the fact that the *Testamentum Domini* lists them first in the hierarchy, but by the *Apostolic Constitutions* the deaconesses have assumed first place. Charles R. Meyer thinks that by the time of the Edict of Theodosius (390) the church had simply expanded too greatly for the widows to do the work assigned to them. This, he thinks, accounts for the rise of the deaconesses.[2]

It was the order of widows, however, and not of the deaconesses, which was the forerunner of monastic orders for women. In our treatment of Tertullian (chap. 5) we noted the potential conflicts between the Christian ideal of virginity and Roman law. Following the Constantinian peace, however, "a woman could be free from entering the bonds of marriage by joining the order of virgins or widows."[3] When asceticism, especially continence, was raised in the "hierarchy of merit," prominence was thereby accorded the widows, who were already pledged to chastity. Various structures developed

114

in the church to accommodate those seeking the ideal of virginity, but the order of widows predated them all and was, thus, the origin of the monastic orders for women that eventually incorporated the earlier women's "offices."[4]

The decline of the widows as an order is directly related to two historical developments: the changing status of ministry in the larger church and the Edict of Constantine (313).

The literary records of early Christianity surveyed here show a progressive decline in the status of women as the church developed and became more institutional. Women exerted more influence during the early period and were increasingly restricted as time went on. The widows are but a case in point of this general trend. In the ministry of Jesus, for example, widows represent the new system of values breaking into the world. They are elevated to prominence by virtue of their spiritual example. They show how God "has put down the mighty from their thrones, and exalted those of low degree" (Luke 1:52).

Likewise, Paul gives the ideal for Christian community relations in Gal. 3:28: neither male nor female in Christ Jesus. Paul assumes women take public roles in worship, as demonstrated by the Corinthian women who prayed and prophesied in that congregation (1 Cor. 11:5). By the early second century, the pastoral writer, as he lays down qualifications for church officials, must also limit an existing, rapidly growing order of women.

Max Weber once pointed out that movements which begin with a charismatic leadership must undergo a process of routinization into a hierarchically organized and self-sustaining social system.[5] We see exactly this process in the development of the church's ministry. B. H. Streeter has observed that the later Pauline epistles give growing importance to a regularized ministry. The movement is away from 1 Corinthians, where prominence in the church depends on personal possession of a spiritual gift, and toward the importance attached to the holding of an office invested with recognized authority.[6] We move from shepherds (*poimēnēs*) to bishops (*episkopoi*). As we noted, the reasons for centralizing authority in offices included the objectives of strengthening the unity of congregations and checking heresy (threats to the church from within). By the time of the letters of Ignatius, we see the single bishop of monepiscopacy as the leading figure in a church, with other offices of ministry hierarchically arranged under his authority.

The institution of widowhood was severely limited when a shift in church policy moved the primary qualification for ministry *from* charism *to* office. While some might argue that the widows are the bridge between the two forms of ministry, this study contends that they in fact represent the continuance of the earlier apostolic understanding of charismatic leadership. Thus, for example, when Montanism with its enthusiasms became a threat to orthodoxy, the widows, although orthodox in belief, became suspect because of their charismatic form of leadership. Because of the charismatic form of their ministry, they were not sufficiently under the control of the hierarchy, so their power was transferred to the more clerical order of deaconesses.[7]

In discussing the *Didascalia Apostolorum* MacKinnon notes that the old charismatic spirit survived in the widows and their supporters, and "one object of the writer is to stamp out what remains of this spirit in the community. . . . There is a tendency to curb these troublesome females by the deaconesses, who . . . are the close associates of the bishop in pastoral work."[8] In ancient Christianity, then, the death of the ideals of widowhood parallel the death of *charisma*.[9] When the church's ministry moved from *Beruf* to *Amt*, the widows and women generally were excluded from office.

This movement cannot really be appreciated apart from the far-reaching implications for the church of the Edict of Constantine. In the coarsest terms, the edict made Christianity "socially acceptable." The problems of the church shifted from those of an oppressed minority to those of an institution assimilating and instructing thousands of new converts. The church's political legitimacy led to economic prosperity, even worldliness. (It was this movement that many think led to the rise of monasticism in the fourth century.) Within the church, as ritual and liturgy became more elaborate, the distinctions between clergy and laity were sharpened. The most critical assessment of the imperial church would assert that its spiritual vigor began to erode as concern for the aims of the kingdom were subjected to the aims of the empire. Until recently, Western history has largely been the story of this jockeying for position in political alliances between church and state.

The move toward an imperial church served to constrict the leadership roles available to women. We noted how equality within the early Christian communities threatened the Roman social order. Now, in order to maintain "social respectability," the church assumed the cultural patterns of the East Roman Empire. As we intimated in our treatment of the pastoral epistles (chap. 3), when the church moved from its foundation in the private sphere of the house (*oikos*) to the public sphere of the city-state (*polis*), women were increasingly excluded from offices of authority in the church.

In a sense, the order of widows was a victim of church history. The demise of the widows is a case in point of what can happen when the church appropriates the values and cultural patterns of the larger society and loses its vocation as "holy" (set apart). In spite of women's lower status in their societies, they were better off in the primitive church than in its institutional successors. As the order of widows demonstrates (and the modern church has discovered), in the final analysis it is impossible to "regularize" the "gifts of the spirit." Those endowed with gifts for ministry found, and still find, ways to use them in spite of official opposition or institutional disapproval. In the case of the widows, we must raise the question, Was the alleged "misbehavior" to which our writers alluded actually a calling to a more active life in the church community and an assertive reaction to the constriction of the widows' roles and responsibilities?

In her earliest days, the primitive church recognized the truth of the prophet Joel's description of the "day of the Lord": "I will pour out my Spirit on *all* people. Your sons *and* daughters will prophesy" (Joel 2:28, italics mine; cf. Acts 2). Perhaps it is time to look back to our roots as a church. In the words of the apostle Paul, "If we live by the Spirit, let us also walk by the Spirit" (Gal. 5:25).

Abbreviations

ANF	Ante-Nicene Fathers
CAH	*Cambridge Ancient History*
DA	*Didascalia Apostolorum*
FRLANT	Forschungen zur Religion und Literatur des Alten und Neuen Testaments
HBD	*Harper's Bible Dictionary*
ICC	International Critical Commentary
IDB	*Interpreter's Dictionary of the Bible*
IDBSup	Supplementary volume to *Interpreter's Dictionary of the Bible*
JBL	*Journal of Biblical Literature*
LCC	Library of Christian Classics
LCL	Loeb Classical Library
TDNT	*Theological Dictionary of the New Testament*
USQR	*Union Seminary Quarterly Review*

Notes

1. THE WIDOWS

1. Francis Brown et al., *Hebrew and English Lexicon to the Old Testament* (Oxford: Clarendon Press, 1957), 47.

2. Ibid., 48. Cf. Gustav Stählin, "Das Bild der Witwe," *Jahrbuch für Antike und Christentum* 17 (1974): 9.

3. Robert Young, *Analytical Concordance to the Bible* (New York: Funk, 1881), 1053. I am in debt to Dr. Burton B. Thurston, Sr., for analysis of the Hebrew and Aramaic terms.

4. Gustav Stählin, "chēra," *TDNT* 9:440.

5. *Ghē (Indo-European); chērai* (Greek); *viduae* (Latin); *widewe* (Anglo-Saxon); *witwe* (German); *widow* (English).

6. James B. Hurley, *Man and Woman in Biblical Perspective* (Grand Rapids: Zondervan, 1981), 137.

7. Stählin, "chēra," 440.

8. Quoted by Mary L. McKenna in *Women of the Church: Role and Renewal* (New York: P. J. Kenedy & Sons, 1967), 37.

9. Ibid. See also Sarah B. Pomeroy, *Goddesses, Whores, Wives, and Slaves: Women in Classical Antiquity* (New York: Schocken Books, 1975), esp. chap. 7, "Hellenistic Women."

10. Hurley, *Man and Woman*, 137–38.

11. The Greek form is infrequently encountered in epigraphs. By 1930 it had been found three times in inscriptions and three times in patristic literature. See Jean-Baptiste Frey, "La signification des termes monandros et univira, coup d'oeil sur la famille romaine aux premiers siècles de notre ère," *Recherche de science religieuse* 20 (1930): 48–60.

12. Helen McClees, *A Study of Women in Attic Inscriptions* (New York: Columbia Univ. Press, 1920), 31–34. See also Barbara J. MacHaffie, *Her Story: Women in Christian Tradition* (Philadelphia: Fortress Press, 1986), esp. chaps. 1 and 2.

13. Leonard Swidler, "Greco-Roman Feminism and the Reception of the Gospel," in *Traditio-Krisis-Renovatio aus theologischer Sicht,* ed. B. Jaspert and R. Mohr (Marburg: N. G. Elwert, 1976), 47.

14. David Schaps, *Economic Rights of Women in Ancient Greece* (Edinburgh: Univ. Library, 1979), 41.

15. "Be mindful of my father and my mother in the halls even as thou art now, or yet more, while I am far away. But when thou shalt see my son a bearded man, wed whom thou wilt, and leave thy house" (Homer, *The Odyssey*, trans. A. T. Murray [Cambridge: Harvard Univ. Press, 1946], 2:217).

16. W. K. Lacey, *The Family in Classical Greece* (Ithaca, N.Y.: Cornell Univ. Press, 1968), 117.

17. Ibid.

18. Schaps, *Economic Rights*, 18.

19. Lacey, *Family*, 175.

20. Ross S. Kraemer, "Women and the Religions of the Greco-Roman World," *Religious Studies Review* 9/2 (1983): 132. It is also interesting to note that, except for Asklepios, the offerings of Athenian women seem most frequently to have been made to female deities. See McClees, *Study of Women*, 16–28.

21. Swidler, "Greco-Roman Feminism," 45–49. See also idem, *Women in Judaism* (Metuchen, N.J.: Scarecrow Press, 1976), 8–21.

22. Swidler, "Greco Roman Feminism," 48.

23. Joachim Jeremias, *Jerusalem in the Time of Jesus* (Philadelphia: Fortress Press, 1969), appendix 18, "The Social Position of Women," 359–76. For more detailed information on women in society and marriage see Swidler, *Women in Judaism*, chaps. 5 and 6, and the article on "widow" in *HBD*, 1132–33.

24. Several recent studies have shown that prohibitions against women were not universal. The most important of these is Bernadette Brooten's *Women Leaders in the Ancient Synagogue* (Chico, Calif.: Scholars Press, 1982). Using inscriptional and archaeological as well as literary evidence, Brooten discusses women as heads of synagogues, leaders, elders, mothers of synagogues, and priests. She demonstrates that these titles were not honorific but designated women performing the same functions as men with similar titles. She notes, however, that such women were probably exceptions to the rule (see p. 149).

25. G. F. Moore, *Judaism* (Cambridge: Harvard Univ. Press, 1954), 2:120.

26. T. J. Meek, *Hebrew Origins* (New York: Harper & Row, Torchbooks, 1960), 77.

27. Stählin, "chēra," 442–43.

28. Lev. 21:14; Ruth 1:9, 13; Ezek. 44:22.

29. 1 Samuel 25; 2 Samuel 11. By the Roman period, however, it was a common practice for Jewish widows to remarry, and it was a noteworthy mark of devotion to the husband if a widow refused to do so. See H. J. Leon, *The Jews of Ancient Rome* (Philadelphia: Jewish Pub. Soc., 1960), 126ff.

30. Stählin, "chēra," 445.

31. Meek, *Hebrew Origins*, 77. Cf. O. J. Baab, "Widow," *IDB* 4:842; and Hurley, *Man and Woman*, 22–23, 36–38.

32. F. Charles Fensham, "Widow, Orphan, and the Poor in Ancient Near Eastern Legal and Wisdom Literature," *Journal of Near Eastern Studies* 21 (1962): 139.

33. Ibid., 135.

34. This was because the garment was often the only covering at night, so it was not only clothing but protection from the elements (Exod. 22:26–27).

35. Isa. 1:17; Jer. 7:5; 22:3; 49:11; Zech. 7:10; Mal. 3:5.

36. Baab, "Widow," 842.

37. Swidler, *Women in Judaism,* 167–68.

38. Ibid., 24–25. Cf. David Verner, *The Household of God: The Social World of the Pastoral Epistles* (Chico, Calif.: Scholars Press, 1983), 35.

39. Swidler, "Greco-Roman Feminism," 53–54; and Paul Veyne, ed., *A History of Private Life from Pagan Rome to Byzantium* (Cambridge: Harvard Univ. Press, Belknap Press, 1987), 34. See also Pomeroy, *Goddesses,* 149–226.

40. Verner, *Household,* 36–38.

41. The following unflattering portrait is from Juvenal's Sixth Satire:
Even worse is the one who has scarcely sat down at the table
When she starts in on books, with praise for Virgil and pardon
For the way Dido died.

. . . .

No one can get in a word edgewise, not even a lawyer,
No, nor an auctioneer, nor even another woman,
Such is the force of her words.

. . . .

Let there be some things in books she does not understand.
How I hate them,
Women who always go back to the pages of Palaemon's grammar,
Keeping all of the rules, and are pedants enough to be quoting
Verses I never heard.
(*The Satires of Juvenal,* trans. Rolfe Humphries [Bloomington: Indiana Univ. Press, 1958], 81–82)

42. Verner, *Household,* 52. Cf. A. J. Marshall, "Roman Women in the Provinces," *Ancient Society* 6 (1975): 123.

43. The extent of this influence is beautifully displayed in Thornton Wilder's epistolary novel *The Ides of March* (New York: Harper & Row, 1987), which is highly recommended to the reader interested in a colorful and accurate depiction of Roman life in the empire.

44. Verner, *Household,* 76–77. Cf. David Balch, *Let Wives Be Submissive: The Domestic Code in 1 Peter* (Chico, Calif.: Scholars Press, 1981).

45. Verner, *Household,* 81.

46. Marjorie Lightman and William Zeisel, "*Univira:* An Example of Continuity and Change in Roman Society," *Church History* 46 (1977): 19. Cf. "Univira," in Adolf Berger, *Encyclopedic Dictionary of Roman Law* (Philadelphia: American Philosophical Soc., 1953), 751; and Frey, "La signification," 48–60. See also Veyne, ed., *History of Private Life,* 75–77.

47. Frey, "La signification," 55.

48. Lightman and Zeisel, "*Univira*," and Veyne, ed., *History of Private Life*, 40.

49. J. P. V. D. Balsdon, *Roman Women, Their History and Habits* (London: The Bodley Head, 1962. Reprint. New York: Barnes & Noble, 1983), 208.

50. Berger ("Univira," 751), gives Augustus's legislation *Lex iulia de maritandis ordinibus*. Cf. Balsdon, *Roman Women*, 76–77, 221.

51. Balsdon, *Roman Women*, 222; Lightman and Zeisel, "*Univira*," 26–29; and Frey, "La signification," 57.

52. Frey, "La signification," 60.

53. Alkan N. Adler, "Ketubah," in *The Jewish Encyclopedia* (New York: Ktav, c. 1900), 7:472. Cf. Verner, *Household*, 45.

2. WIDOWS IN THE NEW TESTAMENT

1. Because the material in the pastoral letters, especially 1 Tim. 5:3–16, is so crucial to the development of an order for widows, and because it represents a later stage in the development of the church, we shall treat it in a separate section. For the present, we will confine ourselves to the authentic Pauline letters and the Markan and Lukan traditions.

2. Howard C. Kee, *Christian Origins in Sociological Perspective* (Philadelphia: Westminster Press, 1980), 91.

3. Mary Rose D'Angelo, "Women and the Earliest Church," in *Women Priests*, ed. Arlene Swidler and Leonard Swidler (New York: Paulist Press, 1977), 194.

4. Ibid., 192. See also "Women," *HBD*, 1138–41; and index entry on "women" in *A History of Private Life from Pagan Rome to Byzantium*, ed. Paul Veyne (Cambridge: Harvard Univ. Press, Belknap Press, 1987), 670.

5. Louis Weil, "Priesthood in the New Testament," in *To Be a Priest*, ed. Robert E. Terwilliger and Urban Holmes (New York: Crossroad, 1975), 64.

6. W. D. Davies, *Christian Origins and Judaism* (London: Darton, Longman & Todd, 1962), 240.

7. Elisabeth Schüssler Fiorenza, "Word, Spirit, and Power: Women in Early Christian Communities," in *Women of Spirit*, ed. Rosemary R. Ruether and Eleanor McLaughlin (New York: Simon & Schuster, 1979), 31. See also Elisabeth Schüssler Fiorenza, "Women in the Pre-Pauline and Pauline Churches," *USQR* 33/3, 4 (1978): 153–66.

8. André Lemaire, "The Ministries in the New Testament," *Biblical Theology Bulletin* 3/2 (1973): 164.

9. Elaine Pagels, *The Gnostic Gospels* (New York: Random House, 1979). Cf. K. McKey, "Gnosticism, Feminism, and Elaine Pagels," *Theology Today* 37 (1981): 498–502.

10. Schüssler Fiorenza, "Word, Spirit, and Power," 57.

11. Constance F. Parvey, "The Theology and Leadership of Women in the New Testament," in *Religion and Sexism*, ed. Rosemary R. Ruether (New York: Simon & Schuster, 1974), 133.

12. David Balch, *Let Wives Be Submissive: The Domestic Code in 1 Peter* (Chico, Calif.: Scholars Press, 1981); Jouette M. Bassler, "The Widow's Tale: A Fresh Look at 1 Tim. 5:3–16," *JBL* 103 (1984): 23–41; J. E. Crouch, *The Origin and Intention of the Colossian Haustafel*, FRLANT 109 (Göttingen: Vandenhoeck & Ruprecht, 1972); and Elisabeth Schüssler Fiorenza, *In Memory of Her: A Feminist Theological Reconstruction of Christian Origins* (London: SCM Press, 1983). Cf. Verner, *The Household of God: The Social World of the Pastoral Epistles* (Chico, Calif.: Scholars Press, 1983).

13. Parvey, "Theology and Leadership," 146.

14. Bassler, "Widow's Tale," 39.

15. Mary L. McKenna, *Women of the Church: Role and Renewal* (New York: P. J. Kenedy & Sons, 1967), 36.

16. Gustav Stählin, "chēra," *TDNT* 9:452.

17. McKenna, *Women of the Church*, 43ff.; and Parvey, "Theology and Leadership," 123ff.

18. See Parvey, "Theology and Leadership," 123–31.

19. *The New Oxford Annotated Bible* (New York: Oxford Univ. Press, 1977), 1368. See n. on Rom. 7:1–6.

20. For a full discussion of the meaning of *makarios* see *TDNT* 4:362–70. In the Beatitudes, Jesus uses the word in a deeply religious sense. "Such blessedness points to a turning of the tables of Jesus' poor, persecuted disciples when God consummates his kingdom on earth" (Robert H. Gundry, *Matthew: A Commentary on His Literary and Theological Art* [Grand Rapids: Wm. B. Eerdmans, 1982], 68).

21. Stählin, "chēra," 448.

22. Ibid.

23. Cf. Matt. 23:14; Luke 20:45–47.

24. The usual Greek verb "to eat" or "to consume" is *esthiō; katesthiō* in Mark 12:40 suggests to devour or prey upon, in short, to eat as an animal would. The distinction is reflected in the difference between the German *essen* and *fressen*. The latter is used of beasts of prey, never of human beings.

25. Ezra P. Gould, *The Gospel according to St. Mark*, ICC (Edinburgh: T. & T. Clark, 1913), 238.

26. Ibid., 239. Mark does not place vv. 38–40 exactly in the teaching of Jesus. The words occurred "in his teaching," not necessarily in this sequence.

27. Gen. 38:14, 19; cf. Luke 7:12.

28. Gould, *St. Mark*, 239.

29. Stählin, "chēra," 449.

30. In both Mark (12:41–44) and Luke (21:1–4) the story of the widow's mite precedes Jesus' prediction of the temple's destruction. The widow's goodness is compared to the shallowness of the external religiosity of the multitude and the scribes. One cannot fail to see the connection between this event and the downfall of the existing religious order, which has not heeded the spirit of the law.

31. Alfred Plummer, *The Gospel according to St. Luke*, ICC (Edinburgh: T. & T. Clark, 1907).

32. Melanie Morrison, "Jesus and Women," *Sojourners* 9/7 (1980): 11. Cf. Eugene H. Maly, "Women and the Gospel of Luke," *Biblical Theology Bulletin* 10/3 (1980): 99–104.

33. Parvey, "Theology and Leadership," 138–41.

34. Maly, "Women," 103; and Plummer, *St. Luke*, 71. Cf. Raymond E. Brown, "The Presentation of Jesus," *Worship* 51 (1977): 2–11.

35. Maly, "Women," 101; and Parvey, "Theology and Leadership," 139. See Luke 7:2–10; 10:29–37, 38–42; 11:2; 13:10–16. See too 14:2–6, 14, 31–33, 34–35; 15:3–7, 8–10.

36. Quoted by Plummer in *St. Luke*, 73.

37. Joseph M. Baumgarten, "4Q502, Marriage or Golden Age Ritual?" *Journal of Jewish Studies* 34/2 (1983): 125–35.

38. Cf. Plato *Laws* 6.759d.

39. "Monogamia apud ethnicos in summo honore est" ("Exhortation to Chastity," xiii; cf. "On Monogamy," xvi).

40. Plummer, *St. Luke*, 72.

41. Luke 18:3; 1 Tim. 5:5; Mark 12:42; James 1:27.

42. Stählin, "chēra," 451.

43. Plummer, *St. Luke*, 72.

44. The force of the Greek term *esplagchnisthe* is stronger than the RSV's "he had compassion" (7:13). The noun *splagchnon* can mean "entrails," literally "guts." To say that Jesus had a "gut feeling" for this widow would not be far from the connotation of the Greek. We might also note in v. 11 that "his disciples" would include more than the Twelve. Would there have been women in this group, as is suggested by Luke 8:1–3? For the implications of this see Schüssler Fiorenza, "The Twelve," in *Women Priests*, ed. Swidler and Swidler, 114–22.

45. E. J. Tinsley, *The Gospel according to Luke* (Cambridge: Cambridge Univ. Press, 1974), 75.

46. Ibid., 75. See Jer. 31:15; 2 Esd. 9:38–104.

47. Stählin, "chēra," 450.

48. Plummer, *St. Luke*, 412.

49. Stählin, "chēra," 450.

50. Plummer, *St. Luke*, 411.

51. Parvey, "Theology and Leadership," 142.

52. Gustav Stählin, "Das Bild der Witwe," *Jahrbuch für Antike und Christentum* 17 (1974): 5–20.

53. Ibid., 20.

54. Ibid.

55. Schüssler Fiorenza, "Word, Spirit, and Power," 57.

56. Parvey, "Theology and Leadership," 143–44.

57. Mary and the Galilean group (Acts 1:14); Sapphira (5:1); queen of

the Ethiopians (8:27); Tabitha (9:36); Mary (12:12); Rhoda (12:13); Lydia (16:14); Damaris (17:34); Priscilla (18:2, 18); Artemis (19:24, 27, 28, 34); Drusilla (24:24); Bernice (25:13).

58. See Acts 4:6; 5:14; 8:3, 12; 10:1; 16:33; 21:5.

59. Priscilla (Acts 18:26); daughters of Philip (21:9); Tabitha (9:36); Lydia (16:14).

60. See, e.g, F. Jackson and K. Lake, *The Acts of the Apostles* (London: MacMillan & Co., 1933), 4:63–66; Johannes Munck, ed., *The Acts of the Apostles*, Anchor Bible Ser. (Garden City, N.Y.: Doubleday & Co., 1973), 55–57.

61. See Jackson and Lake, *Acts* 5:140, 148–49.

62. Howard Hayes, "Acts and 'Christian Socialism,' " *Christian Standard* 18/41 (1983): 13.

63. Charles C. Ryrie, *The Role of Women in the Church* (Chicago: Moody Press, 1970), 81. This holds true until A.D. 70, when the temple was destroyed.

64. Jackson and Lake, *Acts* 4:64.

65. Munck, *Acts*, 56–57 and appendix 6.

66. McKenna, *Women of the Church*, 39.

67. Ibid., 39–41.

68. Jackson and Lake, *Acts* 4:64.

69. Stählin, "chēra," 451 n. 107. For a provocative reading of Luke 8:1–3 see Ben Witherington, "On the Road with Mary Magdalene, Joanna, Susanna, and Other Disciples," *Zeitschrift für die neutestamentliche Wissenschaft* 70 (1979): 243–48.

70. Jackson and Lake, *Acts* 4:64.

71. Ibid., 111.

72. Ibid.

73. McKenna, *Women of the Church*, 42–43. This possibly is also suggested, although obliquely, by Munck. See Munck, *Acts*, 88.

74. Stählin, "chēra," 451–52.

75. McKenna, *Women of the Church*, 43. Cf. Basil, "Introduction to Ascetical Life," *Morals*, rule 74.

76. Ulbrecht Oepke, "Der Dienst der Frau in der urchristlichen Gemeinde," *Neu allgemeine Missionszeitschrift* 16 (1939): 39–53, 81–86.

77. Ewa Wipszycka, *Les ressources et les activités économiques des églises en Egypte du IVe au VIIIe siècle* (Brussels: Fondation égyptologique Reine Elisabeth, 1972), 114. See esp. chap. 4 ("Les dépenses"), part 5, "L'activité philanthropique."

78. Jackson and Lake, *Acts* 4:109: "Earlier than this *mathētēs* is used only in chapter 6 (again several times in a short space, vv. 1, 2, 7). Its distribution in later chapters is more uniform—eighteen times from 11:26 to 21:16."

79. Walter Bauer, *A Greek-English Lexicon of the New Testament*, 2d ed., rev. and aug. F. W. Gingrich and F. W. Danker (Chicago: Univ. of Chicago Press, 1979), 485–86.

80. Parvey, "Theology and Leadership," 145. Cf. Matt. 10:1–4; Mark 3:13–19; Luke 6:12–16.

81. Schüssler Fiorenza, "The Twelve," 114–22.

82. M. R. James, *The Apocryphal New Testament* (Oxford: Clarendon Press, 1953), 93.

83. J. H. Mouton and G. Milligan, *The Vocabulary of the Greek Testament* (Grand Rapids: Wm. B. Eerdmans, 1980), 385.

84. Ryrie also suggests that as head of a household, Lydia was probably a widow (*Role*, 54). See also W. E. Thomas, "The Place of Women in the Church at Philippi," *Expository Times* 83 (1972): 117–20.

85. Stählin, "chēra," 458–59. See Jer. 51:5; Lam. 1:1; Isa. 49:21.

3. ORIGINS OF THE WIDOWS' ORDER

1. For an excellent survey of these issues see the introduction to A. T. Hanson's *The Pastoral Epistles* (Grand Rapids: Wm. B. Eerdmans, 1982); and Martin Dibelius and Hans Conzelmann, *The Pastoral Epistles*, Hermeneia (Philadelphia: Fortress Press, 1972), 1–10. See also the brief entry "Timothy, First and Second, and Titus," in *HBD*, 1075–76; and Walter Lock, *A Critical and Exegetical Commentary on the Pastoral Epistles*, ICC (Edinburgh: T. & T. Clark, 1924).

2. George A. Denzer, "The Pastoral Letters," in *The Jerome Biblical Commentary*, ed. Raymond E. Brown et al. (Englewood Cliffs, N.J.: Prentice-Hall, 1968), 350–61; Burton Scott Easton, *The Pastoral Epistles* (London: SCM Press, 1948); Fred Gealy, "The Pastoral Epistles," in *Interpreter's Bible* (Nashville: Abingdon Press, 1955), 11:343–554; A. J. B. Higgins, "The Pastoral Epistles," in *Peake's Commentary on the Bible*, ed. M. Black (London: Thomas Nelson & Sons, 1963); and C. K. Barrett, *The Pastoral Epistles*, New Clarendon Bible (Oxford: Clarendon Press, 1963).

3. See C. F. D. Moule, "The Problem of the Pastoral Epistles: A Reappraisal," *Bulletin of the John Rylands Library* 4 (1965): 430–52.

4. Philip Schaff, *History of the Christian Church* (Grand Rapids: Wm. B. Eerdmans, 1968), 1:801.

5. Hanson, *Pastoral Epistles*, 13.

6. The classic study of this question is Hans von Campenhausen's *Polykarp von Smyrna und die Pastoralbriefe* (Heidelburg: Carl Winter Universitätsverlag, 1951). The suggestion is made that in fact Polycarp is the author of the Pastorals.

7. Schaff, *History*, 1:798.

8. Hanson, *Pastoral Epistles*, 51.

9. Hanson suggests that this in itself marks the Pastorals as belonging to a generation after Paul (ibid., 31).

10. André Lemaire, "The Ministries in the New Testament: Recent Research," *Biblical Theology Bulletin* 3/2 (1973): 138. Elisabeth Schüssler Fiorenza suggests that the shift in the second century was not from charismatic

to institutional leadership but from charismatic and communal authority to authority vested in local officers. The basic distinction between forms is between the local and translocal (see *In Memory of Her: A Feminist Reconstruction of Christian Origins* [London, SCM Press, 1983], chap. 8).

11. L. Floor, "Church Order in the Pastoral Epistles," *Neotestamentica* 10 (1976): 84.

12. Lemaire, "Ministries," 160.

13. Ibid., 161.

14. Quoted in ibid. Norbert Brox, "Historische und theologische Probleme der Pastoralbriefe" *Kairos* 11 (1969): 81–94.

15. Before Ignatius the monarchical episcopacy is not clearly attested. After his time, the threefold ministry of bishops, priests, and deacons became universal. See Massey H. Shepherd, Jr., "Presbyters in the Early Church," in *To Be a Priest*, ed. Robert E. Terwilliger and Urban Holmes (New York: Crossroad, 1975), 74. Furthermore, the "situation in the Pastoral Epistles is not entirely clear, but it appears that the churches known to Ignatius have moved at most but a step beyond them" (William R. Schoedel, *A Commentary on the Letters of Ignatius of Antioch*, Hermeneia [Philadelphia: Fortress Press, 1985], 22–23).

16. George H. Tavard, *Women in Christian Tradition* (Notre Dame, Ind.: Univ. of Notre Dame Press, 1973), 33–35.

17. K. A. Strand, "The Rise of the Monarchical Episcopate," *Andrews University Seminary Studies* 4 (1966): 65–68.

18. See, e.g., W. Lütgert, *Die Irrlehrer der Pastoralbriefe* (Gütersloh, 1909); Linda Maloney, "Die Stellung der Frau in der Kirche nach der Auffasung der Pastoralbrief," typescript; Elaine Pagels, *The Gnostic Gospels* (New York: Random House, 1979); and R. McL. Wilson, *Gnosis and the New Testament* (Philadelphia: Fortress Press; Oxford: Basil Blackwell, 1968).

19. In heterodox sects of the later second century the role of women was important, as is evidenced by the place of women in the gnostic Gospels. The Nicolaitans and Naasenes received their doctrines from women. The Gnostics paid special heed to prophetesses. Saint Jerome says that Marcion sent a woman ahead of him to prepare people for his "errors." Women were also extremely prominent in Montanism. See Ross S. Kraemer, "The Conversion of Women to Ascetic Forms of Christianity," *Signs* 6/2 (1980): 298–307; and Roger Gryson, *The Ministry of Women in the Early Church* (Collegeville, Minn.: Liturgical Press, 1976), 15–16.

20. Robert J. Karris, "The Background and Significance of the Polemic of the Pastoral Epistles," *JBL* 92 (1973): 549–64.

21. Hanson, *Pastoral Epistles*, 26.

22. David Verner, *The Household of God: The Social World of the Pastoral Epistles* (Chico, Calif.: Scholars Press, 1983), 64. For more on the household codes see David Balch, *Let Wives Be Submissive: The Domestic Code in 1 Peter* (Chico, Calif.: Scholars Press, 1981); and J. E. Crouch, *The Origin and Intention*

of the Colossian Haustafel, FRLANT 109 (Göttingen: Vandenhoeck & Ruprecht, 1972).

23. Verner, *Household,* 81.

24. This is borne out by material in David M. Scholer, "1 Timothy 2:9–15 and the Place of Women in the Church's Ministry" (Paper delivered at the Evangelical Colloquium on Women and the Bible, Oak Brook, Illinois, October 9–11, 1984).

25. Jouette M. Bassler, "The Widow's Tale: A Fresh Look at 1 Tim. 5:3–16," *JBL* 103 (1984): 36.

26. Much later Saint Jerome noted, "They know by experience what a husband's rule is like, and they prefer their liberty as widows" (*Select Letters of St. Jerome,* trans. F. Wright [London, 1933]). Epistle 22.16 is quoted in Marjorie Lightman and William Zeisel's "*Univira:* An Example of Continuity and Change in Roman Society," *Church History* 46 (1977): 29.

27. Bassler, "Widow's Tale," 38.

28. Ibid., 39–40.

29. Ibid., 34.

30. For this final argument refer to R. H. Connolly, *Didascalia Apostolorum* (Oxford: Clarendon Press, 1929), chap. 14.

31. For an excellent summary of the scholarly discussion see Verner, *Household,* 161–66.

32. Jean Danielou and Henri Marrou, *The First Six Hundred Years,* trans. Vincent Cronin (New York: McGraw-Hill, 1964), 1:118; John Döllinger, *The First Age of Christianity and the Church* (London: Gibbings, 1906), 312; W. H. C. Frend, *The Rise of Christianity* (Philadelphia: Fortress Press, 1984), 411; Gustav Stählin, "chēra," *TDNT* 9:453; Eduard Schweizer, *Church Order in the New Testament* (London: SCM Press, 1961), 86.

33. Alexander Sand, "Witwenstand und Ämterstructuren in den urchristlichen Gemeinden," *Bibel und Leben* 12 (1971): 193. Stählin notes three groups: widows in the family unit, younger widowed women, and "true" widows ("chēra," 453–56).

34. G. M. H. Pelser notes that it would be foolish to assume that the passage deals only with care, for then widows under sixty would be uncared for. See "Women and Ecclesiastical Ministries in Paul," *Neotestimentica* 10 (1976): 105. Charles C. Ryrie notes, "Financial and family status, not age, is the primary qualification for a 'widow indeed' " (*The Role of Women in the Church* [Chicago: Moody Press, 1970], 83).

35. Schüssler Fiorenza, *In Memory of Her,* 310–15; and Verner, *Household,* 166, 181ff. Ryrie believes that the catalogue in 1 Tim. 5:3–16 was to systematize financial matters, "and no doubt it paved the way for the development of orders of ministry among women" (*Role,* 84). See also Dennis R. MacDonald, "Virgins, Widows, and Paul in Second-Century Asia Minor," *SBL 1979 Seminar Papers,* ed. Paul J. Achtemeier (Missoula, Mont.: Scholars Press, 1979), 1:177; and F. C. Synge, "Studies in Texts: 1 Timothy 5:3–16," *Theology* 68 (1965): 200–201.

36. As quoted in Lightman and Zeisel, *"Univira,"* 27, the inscription reads:
RIGINE VENEMERENTI FILIA SUA FECIT
VENE, RIGINE MATRI VIDUAE QUE SEDIT
VIDUA ANNOS LX ET ECLESA
NUMQUA GRAVAVIT, UNIBYRA QUE
VIXIT ANNOS LXXX; MESIS V DIES XXVI
The translation would read, "To well-deserving Rigina her daughter nicely made this stone. Rigina, mother, widow, who remained a widow sixty years and never burdened the church; a *univira* who lived 80 years, 5 months, 26 days."

37. Ernest F. Scott, *The Pastoral Epistles* (New York: Harper & Bros., 1936), 63.

38. Dibelius and Conzelmann, *Pastoral Epistles*, 75; cf. Josephus, *Antiquities* 18.66; and Lightman and Zeisel, *"Univira."*

39. Schüssler Fiorenza, *In Memory of Her*, 312. Schüssler Fiorenza also notes that these younger women may be not "real widows" but unmarried women who were enrolled as widows. (See Ignatius *Smyrnaeans* 13.1: "I greet the households of my brothers with their wives and children, and the virgins called widows" [trans. Schoedel, *Ignatius of Antioch*, 247]).

40. Schüssler Fiorenza, *In Memory of Her*, 312.

41. C. K. Barrett, *The Pastoral Epistles*, 76.

42. Schüssler Fiorenza, *In Memory of Her*, 312.

43. Ibid., 313.

44. Verner, *Household*, 177–78. See also "The Acts of Thecla," as translated by Ross Kraemer in *Maenads, Martyrs, Matrons, Monastics* (Philadelphia: Fortress Press, 1988), item 114; and M. R. James in *Apocryphal New Testament*, 272ff.

45. MacDonald, "Virgins, Widows, and Paul," 169–84.

46. Verner, *Household*, 166.

47. Stählin, "chēra," 453.

48. Hanson, *Pastoral Epistles*, 153.

49. Note that there are clearly women deacons in 1 Tim. 3:11.

50. Verner, *Household*, 163.

51. Schweizer, *Church Order*, 86.

52. Josef Ernst, "Die Witwenregel des ersten Timotheusbriefs," *Theologie und Glaube* 59 (1969): 439. For the most complete discussion of the term see Hans-Werner Bartsch, "Die Witwenregel," in *Studien zu den Pastoralbriefen* (Hamburg, 1965): 117–20.

53. Dibelius and Conzelmann, *Pastoral Epistles*, 73; Ernst, "Witwenregel," 439; Sand, "Witwenstand," 193; Verner, *Household*, 162–63.

54. Barrett, *Pastoral Epistles*, 74; Stählin, "chēra," 456.

55. Dibelius and Conzelmann, *Pastoral Epistles*, 75; cf. Sand, "Witwenstand," 95.

56. Wayne A. Meeks, "The Voluntary Association," in *The First Urban*

Christians: The Social World of the Apostle Paul (New Haven: Yale Univ. Press, 1983), 77–80; and Stählin, "chēra," 456. Cf. Verner, *Household*. For an interesting comparison of church organizations and Greco-Roman clubs see Schüssler Fiorenza, *In Memory of Her*, 287; and Edwin Hatch, *The Organization of the Early Christian Churches* (Oxford: Rivington, 1881).

57. Lock, *Critical and Exegetical Commentary*, 59.

58. Bartsch, "Die Witwenregel," 137.

59. Verner, *Household*, 164.

60. Barrett, *Pastoral Epistles*, 76.

61. Easton, *Pastoral Epistles*, 154.

62. Dibelius and Conzelmann, *Pastoral Epistles*, 75; cf. J. H. Moulton and G. Milligan, *The Vocabulary of the Greek Testament* (Grand Rapids: Wm. B. Eerdmans, 1980), 115–16.

63. Döllinger, *First Age of Christianity*, 312.

64. Gryson, *Ministry of Women in the Early Church*, 9.

65. Rosamond Nugent, *Portrait of the Consecrated Woman in Greek Christian Literature of the First Four Centuries* (Washington, D.C.: Catholic Univ. of America Press, 1941), 1–5.

66. Bartsch, "Die Witwenregel," 128.

67. Easton, *Pastoral Epistles*, 152.

68. Barrett, *Pastoral Epistles*, 75.

69. Jean B. La Porte, "The Elderly in the Life and Thought of the Early Church," in *Ministry with the Aging*, ed. W. M. Clements (San Francisco: Harper & Row, 1981), 38.

70. Stählin, "chēra," 454 n. 131.

71. For a summary of the various readings see Hanson, *Pastoral Epistles*, 77–78. See also C. W. Emmet, "The Husband of One Wife, I Tim. 3.2, 12," *Expository Times* 19 (1907): 39–40; and Stählin, "chēra," 457.

72. Karen Jo Torjesen, "From the Private Sphere of the Hellenistic Household to the Public Sphere of the Imperial Church: Women's Leadership Roles in Transition" (Paper delivered at the Society of Biblical Literature meeting, Anaheim, California, November 24, 1985).

73. Scott, *Pastoral Epistles*, 61.

74. J. Müller-Bardorff, "Zur Exegese von I Tim. 5.3–16," in *Gott und die Götter* (Berlin: Evangelische Verlagsanstalt, 1958), 122.

75. Scott, *Pastoral Epistles*, 61.

76. T. W. Manson, *The Church's Ministry* (London: Hodder & Stoughton, 1948), 27.

77. Hanson, *Pastoral Epistles*, 96.

78. Schweizer, *Church Order*, 86 n. 337.

79. Verner, *Household*, 165.

80. La Porte, "Elderly," 46.

81. Jean B. La Porte, *The Role of Women in Early Christianity* (Lewiston, N.Y.: Edwin Mellen Press, 1982), 58.

82. La Porte, "Elderly," 45. See Eusebius (*Ecclesiastical History* VI.43.11), who in reference to the mid-third-century situation wrote, "More than 1500 widows and persons in distress" were supported by the church in Rome. Cf. Tertullian, "On Penitence," 9.

83. Dibelius and Conzelmann, *Pastoral Epistles*, 75.

84. For a summary of the argument see Hanson, *Pastoral Epistles*, 99. Cf. Müller-Bardorff, "Exegese," 123.

85. Schweizer, *Church Order*, 186. See also G. Lohfink, "Die Normativität der Amtsvorstellungen in den Pastoralbriefen," *Theologische Quartalschrift* 157 (1977): 93–104.

86. "Certain widows were employed as active church-workers and were 'enrolled' as irrevocably dedicated to their duties, which would correspond in large degree to those of the deacons. . . . In I Timothy the functions of the deaconesses are entrusted to the 'enrolled widows' (5.9ff). . . . These widows were deaconesses in every regard but their name" (Easton, *Pastoral Epistles*, 153, 185).

87. G. H. R. Horsley, *New Documents Illustrating Early Christianity* (North Ryde: Austl.: Macquarie Univ. Press, 1981), 121.

88. Quoted by A. Kalsbach in *Die altkirchliche Einrichtung der Diakonissen* (Freiburg im Breisgau: Herder & Co., 1926), 15.

89. Verner, *Household*, 172.

90. Stählin, "chēra," 457.

91. Dorothy Irvin, "The Ministry of Women in the Early Church: The Archaeological Evidence," *Duke Divinity School Review* 45/2 (1980): 76–86. See also Bernadette Brooten, *Women Leaders in the Ancient Synagogue* (Chico, Calif.: Scholars Press, 1982); and, on the later fourth-century situation, Frend, *Rise of Christianity*, 569–70, 588 n. 117.

92. MacDonald, "Virgins, Widows, and Paul," 177.

93. Verner, *Household*, 166.

94. Easton, *Pastoral Epistles*, 185.

4. THE APOSTOLIC PERIOD

1. Jean Danielou and Henri Marrou, *The First Six Hundred Years*, vol. 1, trans. Vincent Cronin (New York: McGraw-Hill, 1964); W. H. C. Frend, *The Early Church* (Philadelphia: Fortress Press, 1982); idem, *The Rise of Christianity* (Philadelphia: Fortress Press, 1984); and B. H. Streeter, *The Primitive Church* (London: MacMillan & Co., 1929).

2. Streeter, *Primitive Church*, 47.

3. Phillip Schaff, *History of the Christian Church* (Grand Rapids: Wm. B. Eerdmans, 1970), 2:46; cf. Frend, *Rise of Christianity*, 161–92.

4. Frend, *Early Church*, 58–71; cf. idem, *Rise of Christianity*, 161–228.

5. Schaff, *History* 2:57.

6. Cecil J. Cadoux, *The Early Church and the World* (Edinburgh: T. & T. Clark, 1925); cf. Frend, *Rise of Christianity*, 234–44.

7. S. L. Davies, *The Revolt of the Widows* (Carbondale: Southern Illinois Univ. Press, 1980), 11.

8. Davies, *Revolt of the Widows*, chaps. 6 and 7.

9. See Dennis MacDonald, "Virgins, Widows, and Paul in Second Century Asia Minor," in *SBL 1979 Seminar Papers*, ed. Paul Achtemeier (Missoula, Mont.: Scholars Press, 1979), 1:169–84.

10. Ross S. Kraemer, "The Conversion of Women to Ascetic Forms of Christianity," *Signs* 6/2 (1980): 298–307; cf. idem, ed., *Maenads, Martyrs, Matrons, Monastics* (Philadelphia: Fortress Press, 1988).

11. Elaine Pagels, *The Gnostic Gospels* (New York: Random House, 1979). For criticism of Pagels's opinions see K. McKey, "Gnosticism, Feminism, and Elaine Pagels," *Theology Today* 37 (1981): 498–502; and R. J. Hoffman, "De Statu Feminarum," *Eglise et Théologie* 14 (1983): 298–304.

12. See, e.g., Philip Carrington, *The Early Christian Church: The Second Century* (Cambridge: Cambridge Univ. Press, 1957) 1:187ff.; E. Dassmann, *Der Stachel im Fleisch: Paulhus in der früchristlichen Literatur bis Irenaeus* (Münster, 1979); Dennis R. MacDonald, *The Legend and the Apostle: The Battle for Paul in Story and Canon* (Philadelphia: Westminster Press, 1983); W. Schneemelcher, "Die Acta Pauli—neue Funde und neue Aufgaben," *Theologische Literaturzeitung* 89 (1964): 241–54. See also Richard I. Pervo, *Profit with Delight: The Literary Genre of the Acts of the Apostles* (Philadelphia: Fortress Press, 1987).

13. Cyril C. Richardson et al., *Early Christian Fathers*, LCC (Philadelphia: Westminster Press, 1953), 35. For an English translation of *1 Clement* see pp. 43–73.

14. Ibid., 37.

15. Kirsopp Lake, ed., *Apostolic Fathers*, 2 vols., LCL (Cambridge: Harvard Univ. Press, 1977), 1:23. Unless otherwise noted, quotations from the Apostolic Fathers in the text are from Lake's translation.

16. For a discussion of the problem see Frend, *Early Church*, 37ff. On Ignatius's letters in general, see William R. Schoedel, *A Commentary on the Letters of Ignatius of Antioch*, Hermeneia (Philadelphia: Fortress Press, 1985).

17. See W. Telfer, *The Office of a Bishop* (London, 1962), chap. 2.

18. Richardson, *Early Christian Fathers*, 76.

19. For a brief history of the textual questions see ANF 1:45–48; Lake, *Apostolic Fathers* 1:166–71; and Schoedel, *Ignatius of Antioch*, 3–7.

20. ANF 1:82.

21. Ibid., 92. On Zahn's solution to this problem see Schoedel, *Ignatius of Antioch*, 65.

22. Richardson, *Early Christian Fathers*, 116. C. H. Turner concurs, following Lightfoot's exegesis of *Smyrnaeans* 13: "those whom we call in the Church widows and who are really also virgins" ("Ministries of Women in the Primitive Church," *Constructive Quarterly* 7 [1919]: 439).

23. Mary L. McKenna, *Women of the Church* (New York: Kenedy Co., 1967), 50.

24. Roger Gryson, *The Ministry of Women in the Early Church* (Collegeville, Minn.: Liturgical Press, 1976), 13; cf. chap. 2, n. 18.

25. See G. Delling, "parthenos," *TDNT* 5:826–37; René Metz, *La consécration des vierges dans l'église romaine* (Paris: Presses Universitaires de France, 1954), 45; J. H. Moulton and G. Milligan, *The Vocabulary of the Greek Testament* (Grand Rapids: Wm. B. Eerdmans, 1980), 494; and Joseph H. Thayer, *Greek-English Lexicon of the New Testament* (New York: Harper & Bros., 1889), 489. For a discussion of the widow/virgin/deaconess question see A. Kalsbach, *Die altkirchliche Einrichtung der Diakonissen* (Freiburg im Breisgau: Herder & Co., 1926), 100ff.

26. Donald MacKenzie, "Virgins," *Dictionary of the Apostolic Church*, ed. James Hastings (New York: Charles Scribner's Sons, 1918), 2:640, 642.

27. William Smith and Samuel Cheetham, eds., *A Dictionary of Christian Antiquities* (Hartford: J. B. Burr, 1880), 2:2033. Cf. Schoedel, *Ignatius of Antioch*, 269.

28. See Richardson's introduction to the letter of Polycarp in *Early Christian Fathers*, 121–30.

29. W. E. Thomas, "The Place of Women in the Church at Philippi," *Expository Times* 83 (1972): 120.

30. Ibid., 119.

31. Moulton and Milligan, *Vocabulary*, 623.

32. Gryson, *Ministry of Women*, 12.

33. Turner, "Ministries of Women," 438.

34. For a gloss on this point, see the discussion of sins of the tongue in Eph. 4:25—5:20 and James 3.

35. Carolyn Osiek, "Widow as Altar: Rise and Fall of a Symbol," *Second Century* 3/3 (1983): 159–69.

36. Ibid., 166.

37. Turner, "Ministries of Women," 438.

38. Smith and Cheetham, eds., *Dictionary of Christian Antiquities*, 2033. See also Osiek: "The original basis for associating widow and altar . . . is the depositing of the gifts of the faithful upon the altar and their distribution to widows as recipients of charity" ("Widow as Altar," 166).

39. G. W. H. Lampe, *Patristic Greek Lexicon* (Oxford: Clarendon Press, 1968), 660.

40. Jean B. La Porte, *The Role of Women in Early Christianity* (Lewiston, N.Y.: Edwin Mellen Press, 1982), 60.

41. Thomas, "Place of Women," 120.

42. Gryson, *Ministry of Women*, 12–13.

43. Lake, *Apostolic Fathers* 2:3.

44. Ibid. 2:285.

45. Ibid. 2:25.

46. Gryson, *Ministry of Women*, 14.

47. Leopold Zscharnack, *Der Dienst der Frau in den ersten Jahrhunderten der christlichen Kirche* (Göttingen, 1902), 105.

48. J. G. Davies, "Deacons, Deaconesses, and the Minor Orders in the Patristic Period," *Journal of Ecclesiastical History* 14 (1963): 4.

49. Ibid., 5.

50. La Porte, *Role of Women*, 60.

51. Robert Frick, "Diakonie," in *Evangelisches Kirchenlexikon*, ed. R. Frick et al. (Göttingen: Vandenhoeck & Ruprecht, 1956), 922.

52. For a fuller discussion of the correspondence see Frend, *Early Church*, 44ff.

53. Quoted by Charles C. Ryrie in *The Role of Women in the Church* (Chicago: Moody Press, 1970), 102: " *'Necessarium credidi ex duabus ancillis quae ministrae dicebantur, quid esset veri et per tormenta quaerere'* (necessary to inquire into the real truth of the matter by subjecting to torture two female slaves, who were called deacons). In this sentence, *ancilla* is a term designating the social condition of these women, and *ministra* a title given to them by the Christians. It is probable, although not absolutely certain, that the Greek word *diakonos* corresponds to the Latin *ministra*." See Gryson, *Ministry of Women*, 15.

54. Johannes Leipoldt, *Die Frau in der antiken Welt und Urchristentum* (Gütersloh: Gerd Mohn, 1962), 133.

55. Quoted by Turner in "Ministries of Women," 439. Cf. Lucian, *The Passing of Peregrinus*, LCL 5:12.

56. Gryson, *Ministry of Women*, 14.

5. TERTULLIAN OF CARTHAGE

1. B. H. Streeter, *The Primitive Church* (London: Macmillan & Co., 1929), 53; and W. H. C. Frend, *The Early Church* (Philadelphia: Fortress Press, 1982), 72–84.

2. For the trial account of Carthaginean Christian women and men see "The Martyrs of Scilli" in *Maenads, Martyrs, Matrons, Monastics*, ed. Ross S. Kraemer (Philadelphia, Fortress Press, 1988), item 122.

3. Frend, *Early Church*, 79; cf. idem, *Martyrdom and Persecution in the Early Church* (Garden City, N.Y.: Doubleday & Co., 1965), esp. chap. 12.

4. See "The Martyrdom of Perpetua," in *A Lost Tradition: Women Writers of the Early Church*, ed. and trans. Patricia Wilson-Kastner et al. (Lanham, Md.: Univ. Press of America, 1981), 19–30.

5. Hans Lietzmann, *History of the Early Church*, trans. Bertram L. Woolf (London: Lutterworth Press, 1938; reprint, 1961), 2:216.

6. Lietzmann, *History* 2:219.

7. See ANF 3:4ff.

8. Charles C. Ryrie, *The Role of Women in the Church* (Chicago: Moody Press, 1970), 114.

9. Frend, *Early Church*, 70.

10. On Montanism, see Frend, *Early Church;* idem, *The Rise of Christianity* (Philadelphia: Fortress Press, 1984); Lietzmann, *History*, vol. 2, chap. 8; and G. L. Prestige, *Fathers and Heretics* (London: SPCK, 1954).

11. Tertullian, "On the Veiling of Virgins," in ANF 4:27ff.

12. Archibald Robertson and Alfred Plummer, *The First Epistle of St. Paul to the Corinthians*, ICC (Edinburgh: T. & T. Clark, 1911), 230. See also Gerd Theissen, *Psychological Aspects of Pauline Theology* (Philadelphia: Fortress Press, 1987). See also Cynthia L. Thompson, "Hairstyles, Head-coverings, and St. Paul: Portraits from Corinth," *Biblical Archaeologist* 51 (1988): 98-115.

13. W. M. Ramsay, *The Cities of St. Paul* (London: Hodder & Stoughton, 1907), 204–5.

14. Cf. Acts 2:18; 21:9.

15. Tertullian, "On the Veiling of Virgins," 33.

16. Roger Gryson, *The Ministry of Women in the Early Church* (Collegeville, Minn.: Liturgical Press, 1976), 19.

17. Tertullian, "On the Veiling of Virgins," 27.

18. James Hastings, ed., *A Dictionary of the Bible* (New York: Charles Scribner's Sons, 1905), 4:848.

19. Tertullian, "On the Veiling of Virgins," 33.

20. Ibid.

21. Ibid.

22. Ibid.

23. In ANF 4:67.

24. Gryson, *Ministry of Women*, 21.

25. ANF 4:86.

26. Jean B. La Porte, *The Role of Women in Early Christianity* (Lewiston, N.Y.: Edwin Mellen Press, 1982), 126.

27. ANF 18:85.

28. Arthur J. Maclean, *The Ancient Church Orders* (Cambridge: Cambridge Univ. Press, 1910), 17, 83. See also La Porte, *Role of Women,* 127.

29. Helena Wylde Swiny, *An Archaeological Guide to the Ancient Kourion Area* (Nicosia: Zavallis Press, 1982), 119. Also helpful in this regard is J. G. Davies's *The Origin and Development of Early Christian Church Architecture* (London: SCM Press, 1952).

30. This observation arises from looking at the excavations at Kurion in March 1985. I am grateful to the Department of Antiquities in Cyprus for the courtesy of an archaelogical pass and to the Cyprus-American Archaeological Research Institute for use of their library.

31. Tertullian, "On the Veiling of Virgins," 33.

32. Tertullian, "Exhortation to Chastity," in ANF 4:50.

33. Ibid., 55.

34. Ibid., 56.

35. Ibid.

36. Ibid.

37. Strange as it may seem to us, such "spiritual marriages" were prevalent at some periods in the church. At least two of the Apostolic Fathers, John Chrysostom and Saint Jerome, object to them not only on the basis of the

scandal they caused in the larger community, but because by means of them the woman sacrificed her freedom. Jerome specifically notes that women are "enslaved" by the arrangement. For more on the practice of spiritual marriage, see Elizabeth A. Clark, "Ascetic Renunciation and Feminine Advancement: A Paradox of Late Ancient Christianity," *Anglican Theological Review* 63/3 (1981): 240–57; idem, "John Chrysostom and Subintroductae," *Church History* 46 (1977): 170–85.

38. Jo Ann McNamara, "Wives and Widows in Early Christian Thought," *International Journal of Women's Studies* 2/6 (1979): 488.

39. ANF 4:58.

40. Cf. Gryson's reading of this passage (*Ministry of Women*, 20–21).

41. Rosamond Nugent, *Portrait of the Consecrated Woman in the Greek Christian Literature of the First Four Centuries* (Washington, D.C.: Catholic Univ. of America Press, 1941), 1–2.

42. McNamara, "Wives and Widows," 576.

43. Ibid.

44. Cecil J. Cadoux, *The Early Church and the World* (Edinburgh: T. & T. Clark, 1925), 282. On celibacy in the third century see Frend, *Rise of Christianity*, 411–12.

45. McNamara, "Wives and Widows," 584.

46. Ibid.

47. The fact that Callistus (bishop of Rome, 217–222) pronounced marriages across social lines legal in the eyes of the church indicates the extent of the church's departure from Roman law as well as consciousness of its independence and power in Rome. See Cadoux, *Early Church and World*, 443ff.

48. McNamara, "Wives and Widows," 584.

49. Nugent, *Portrait of Consecrated Women*, 5.

50. McNamara, "Wives and Widows," 576.

51. S. L. Davies, *The Revolt of the Widows* (Carbondale: Southern Illinois Univ. Press, 1980), chap. 6.

52. Ross S. Kraemer, "The Conversion of Women to Ascetic Forms of Christianity," *Signs* 6/2 (1980): 298–307.

53. Jo Ann McNamara, "Sexual Equality and the Cult of Virginity in Early Christian Thought," *Feminist Studies* 3 (1976): 151.

54. Clark, "Ascetic Renunciation and Feminine Advancement," 240.

55. Davies, *Revolt of the Widows*, 114.

56. We should simply note again that many writers felt and still feel that "the pre-eminence of women as evangelists or prophets or teachers is obviously a characteristic of the heresies" (Philip Carrington, *The Early Christian Church: The Second Century* [Cambridge: Cambridge Univ. Press, 1957], 2:299).

57. Tertullian, "To His Wife," in ANF 4:39.

58. Ibid., 41.

59. See McNamara, "Wives and Widows," 587–88.

60. Recall the discussion of the term *monandros* (see chap. 1 above).

61. Tertullian, "To His Wife," 42–43.

62. Ibid., 43.

63. Pamelii et al., eds., *Patrologiae Cursus Completus, Tertulliana* (Paris, 1844), 1:1286: "Apostoli declarat, cum digamos non sinit praesidere, cum viduam allegi in ordinem nisi univiram non concedit."

64. Tertullian, "To His Wife," 43.

65. For a discussion of the 1 Timothy passage, see C. W. Emmet, "The Husband of One Wife, I Tim. 3.2, 12," *Expository Times* 19 (1907): 39–40.

66. McNamara, "Wives and Widows," 587.

67. Tertullian, "To His Wife," 43.

68. Ibid.

69. Leopold Zscharnack, *Der Dienst der Frau in den ersten Jahrhunderten der christlichen Kirche* (Göttingen, 1902), 109.

70. A letter of Cornelius, Bishop of Rome (d. A.D. 253), lists "more than 1500 widows and persons in distress" with the clergy in Rome. See Eusebius *Ecclesiastical History* VI.43.11. Cf. chap. 3, n. 81, above.

71. Mary L. McKenna, *Women of the Church: Role and Renewal* (New York: P. J. Kenedy & Sons, 1967), 52.

72. Cadoux, *Early Church and World*, 443.

73. Zscharnack, *Der Dienst der Frau*, 110.

74. McKenna, *Women of the Church*, 52–53.

6. THE WIDOWS IN THE THIRD CENTURY

1. Phillip Schaff, *History of the Christian Church*, vol. 2 (Grand Rapids: Wm. B. Eerdman's, 1968); S. A. Cook et al., and *CAH* 12. See also W. H. C. Frend, *The Rise of Christianity* (Philadelphia: Fortress Press, 1984), esp. chap. 12, "Church and People in the Third Century."

2. See Colin McEvedy, *The Penguin Atlas of Ancient History* (Harmondsworth: Penguin Books, 1967), 84–90.

3. A. Alföldi, "The Crisis of the Empire (A.D. 249–279)," in *CAH* 12:194.

4. See N. H. Baynes, "The Great Persecution," chap. 19 in *CAH* 12; W. H. C. Frend, *The Early Church* (Philadelphia: Fortress Press, 1982), 115–25; idem, *Martyrdom and Persecution*, chap. 13; idem, *Rise of Christianity*, 318–28.

5. J. E. L. Oulton, *Eusebius: The Ecclesiastical History*, 2 vols., LCL (Cambridge: Harvard Univ. Press, 1953), 2:257.

6. Hans Lietzmann, *From Constantine to Julian*, vol. 3 of *History of the Early Church*, trans. Bertram L. Woolf (London, Lutterworth Press, 1938. Reprint 1961), 71.

7. Cecil J. Cadoux, *The Early Church and the World* (Edinburgh: T. & T. Clark, 1925), 597; cf. Frend, *Rise of Christianity*, 411–14.

8. Oulton, *Eusebius* 2:103, 107.

9. Mary L. McKenna, *Women of the Church: Role and Renewal* (New York: P. J. Kenedy & Sons, 1967), 51.

10. See Jean Danielou and Henri Marrou, *The First Six Hundred Years* (New York: McGraw-Hill, 1964), 1:163.

11. See Roger Gryson, *The Ministry of Women in the Early Church* (Collegeville, Minn.: Liturgical Press, 1976), 25–34.

12. Ibid., 28.

13. Origen, *Commentary on John*, quoted in ibid., 26.

14. Ibid., 27.

15. Ibid.

16. Quoted in ibid., 29. See Origen *Fragments on 1 Corinthians* in ANF.

17. Gryson, *Ministry of Women*, 32.

18. Origen *Commentary on Romans 10.20*, quoted in ibid., 27–28.

19. The *DA* is also known as the Catholic Teaching of the Twelve Apostles and Holy Disciples of our Saviour. See Johannes Quasten, *Patrology* (Westminster, Md.: Newman Press, 1953), 2:147–52.

20. The *Apostolic Constitutions* devotes section 1 of book 3 to the widows. Some of that material is clearly from the *DA*.

21. Gryson, *Ministry of Women*, 134–35.

22. Ibid., 39.

23. Quasten, *Patrology* 2:149. For a summary of the material on widows in the *DA* see Jean B. La Porte, *The Role of Women in Early Christianity* (Lewiston, N.Y.: Edwin Mellen Press, 1982), 60–64.

24. Beginning with the *DA* and in most of the church orders, the deaconesses figure prominently as ecclesiastical functionaries. In the course of the third and fourth centuries they take precedence over the widows and, in fact, are given authority over them. The development of the order of deaconesses is important and interesting but outside the scope of this study. For information on this development, see J. G. Davies, "Deacons, Deaconesses, and the Minor Orders in the Patristic Period," *Journal of Ecclesiastical History* 14 (1963): 1–15; Jean Danielou, "Le ministére des femmes dans l'église ancienne," *La maison-Dieu* 61/1 (1960): 70–96; Robert Frick, "Weibliche Diakonie," in *Evangelisches Kirchenlexikon* (1956) 1:922; F. J. Leenhardt and F. Blanke, *Die Stellung der Frau in NT und in der alten Kirche* (Zurich: Zwingli Verlag, 1949); C. R. Meyer, "Ordained Women in the Early Church," *Chicago Studies* 4/3 (1965): 285–308; J. Viteau, "La Institution des diacres et des Veuves," *Revue d'Histoire Ecclésiastique* 22 (1929): 513–37; and Leopold Zscharnack, *Der Dienst der Frau in den ersten Jahrhunderten der christlichen Kirche* (Göttingen, 1902), 105.

25. R. Hugh Connolly, ed. *Didascalia Apostolorum* (Oxford: Clarendon Press, 1929), 88. All references to the *DA* are to this edition.

26. Ibid., 120.

27. Ibid., 130.

28. Ibid., xliii.

29. Ibid., xliii, 131.

30. Ibid., 156–57: "Episcopi ergo et diacones, obseruate altario Christi, id

est uiduis et orfanis, cum omni diligentia, curam facientes de his quae ac-
cipiuntur cum scrupulositate, qualis est ille qui dat, aut illa quae dat, ut
adescentur. Iterum adque iterum dicimus, quoniam altare de laboribus ius-
titiae accipere debet."

31. Ibid., 158–59.
32. Ibid., 159.
33. Ibid., 88.
34. Ibid., 138, 140.
35. Discussed by Gryson in *Ministry of Women*, 37–38.
36. *DA*, 132.
37. Ibid., 134.
38. Ibid., 134; cf. Matt. 18:19.
39. *DA*, 136.
40. Ibid., 142.
41. Ibid., 138, 140.
42. Gryson, *Ministry of Women*, 140. See *DA*, 145.
43. *DA*, 138.
44. Charles C. Ryrie, *The Role of Women in the Church* (Chicago: Moody
Press, 1970), 132.
45. *DA*, 138.
46. Ibid., 133.
47. Ibid., 132.
48. Ibid., 142.
49. Ibid., 132ff.
50. Ibid., 132.
51. Ibid., 134.
52. Gryson, *Ministry of Women*, 37.
53. *DA*, 133–34.
54. On 1 Tim. 5:3–16 see chap. 3 above.
55. *DA*, 136, 138.
56. Ibid., 142.
57. Ibid., 143.
58. F. X. Funk, *Didascalia et Constitutiones Apostolorum*, 2 vols. (Paderborn,
1905; reprint, Turin, 1964).
59. *DA*, 143.
60. Ibid., 143.
61. Ibid., 133.
62. Ibid., 134.
63. Ibid., 143.
64. Ibid., 158–59.
65. Ibid., 88.
66. Kirsopp Lake, ed., *Apostolic Fathers*, 2 vols., LCL (Cambridge: Harvard
Univ. Press, 1977), 1:288–89.
67. Carolyn Osiek, "Widow as Altar: Rise and Fall of a Symbol," *Second
Century* 3/3 (1983): 159–69.

68. Davies, "Deacons, Deaconesses, and the Minor Orders," 5.

69. Gryson, *Ministry of Women*, 40–41.

70. James MacKinnon, *From Christ to Constantine* (London: Longmans, Green & Co., 1936), 315.

71. MacKinnon, *From Christ to Constantine*, 315; McKenna, *Women of the Church*, 52–53.

72. See McKenna, *Women of the Church*, chap. 6, esp. 111–16.

7. THE WIDOW AS ALTAR

1. ANF 4:43.

2. *DA*, 88.

3. Ibid., 133.

4. Ibid., 134.

5. Ibid., 143.

6. Ibid., 159.

7. ANF 18:59.

8. This suggestion is also found in Ignatius's *Letter to the Magnesians* VI (see Kirsopp Lake, ed., *Apostolic Fathers* [Cambridge: Harvard Univ. Press, 1977], 1:200–203) and indicates a first-century origin for metaphorical thinking about church offices.

9. *The Writings of Methodius*, ANF 6:328. The brazen altar was the large, stationary altar in front of the temple in Jerusalem. The golden altar or incense altar was much smaller and was originally in the wilderness sanctuary.

10. See Carolyn Osiek, "The Widows as Altar: Rise and Fall of a Symbol," *Second Century* 3/3 (1983): 159–69.

11. Everett Ferguson, *Early Christians Speak* (Austin, Tex.: Sweet Pub. Co., 1971), 122.

12. Mary L. McKenna, *Women of the Church: Role and Renewal* (New York: P. J. Kenedy & Sons, 1967), 51.

13. T. H. Gaster, "Sacrifices and Offerings," *IDB* 4:147, 159.

14. Lake, *Apostolic Fathers* 1:331.

15. *Clement of Alexandria*, ANF 2:428.

16. ANF 4:505.

17. Lake, *Apostolic Fathers* 1:79; Cyril C. Richardson et al., *Early Christian Fathers*, LCC (Philadelphia: Westminster Press, 1953), 133.

18. Jean B. La Porte, *The Role of Women in Early Christianity* (Lewiston, N.Y.: Edwin Mellen Press, 1982), 60.

19. W. E. Thomas, "The Place of Women in the Church at Philippi," *Expository Times* 83 (1972): 120.

20. See Matt. 5:23; 23:35; Luke 1:11; Rom. 11:3; l Cor. 9:13; 10:18; Heb. 7:13; 13:10; James 2:21; Rev. 6:9; 8:3.

21. David E. Garland, *The Intention of Matthew 23* (Leiden: E. J. Brill, 1979), 132–36.

22. F. F. Bruce, "Altar, N. T.," in *IDB Sup*, 19.

23. Hans von Campenhausen et al., eds., *Die Religion in Geschichte und Gegenwart*, 3d ed. (Tübingen: J. C. B. Mohr [Paul Siebeck], 1957), 1:255.

24. See G. W. H. Lampe, *Patristic Greek Lexicon* (Oxford: Clarendon Press, 1968), 660.

25. Jouette M. Bassler, "The Widow's Tale: A Fresh Look at 1 Tim. 5:3–16," *JBL* 103 (1984):36.

26. For an interesting study of how women have turned the negative aspects of institutional Christianity into positive spiritual results, see Sandra M. Schneiders, "The Effects of Women's Experience on Their Spirituality," *Spirituality Today* 35/2 (1983): 100–116.

EPILOGUE

1. J. G. Davies, "Deacons, Deaconesses, and the Minor Orders in the Patristic Period," *Journal of Ecclesiastical History* 14 (1963): 1–4.

2. C. R. Meyer, "Ordained Women in the Early Church," *Chicago Studies* 4/3 (1965): 288–93.

3. George H. Tavard, *Women in Christian Tradition* (Notre Dame, Ind.: Univ. of Notre Dame Press, 1973), 78.

4. For a fine study on the movement from ancient women's orders to monastic institutions see René Metz, *La consécration des vierges dans l'église romaine* (Paris: Presses Universitaires de France, 1954).

5. See Max Weber, *The Sociology of Religion* (1922; Boston: Beacon Press, 1964).

6. B. H. Streeter, *The Primitive Church* (London: Macmillan & Co., 1929), 80–83. See also Eduard Schweizer, *Church Order in the New Testament* (London: SCM Press, 1961).

7. Mary L. McKenna, *Women of the Church: Role and Renewal* (New York: P. J. Kenedy & Sons, 1967), 118.

8. James MacKinnon, *From Christ to Constantine* (London: Longmans, Green & Co., 1936), 315.

9. A. Kalsbach, *Die altkirchliche Einrichtung der Diakonissen* (Freiburg im Breisgau: Herder & Co., 1926), 96.